Matt Preston is Australia's foremost authority on delicious and achievable food, thanks to his role as co-host and judge on *MasterChef Australia* and his regular columns in News Ltd's *Taste* food supplement, *delicious* magazine and *Taste* magazine.

Matt is the author of three bestselling cookbooks: *Matt Preston's 100 Best Recipes* (2012), *Fast, Fresh and Unbelievably Delicious* (2013) and *Cook Book* (2014).

THE SIMPLE
SECRETS

TO COOKING EVERYTHING BETTER

This book is dedicated to Marnie and Kate,
because you are the best and none of my cookbooks would
have been anywhere near as good without you.

You inspire me, you awe me, but above all
you constantly make me go 'yum'!
Thankyou for everything!

THE
SIMPLE
SECRETS

TO COOKING EVERYTHING BETTER

MATT PRESTON

plum. Pan Macmillan Australia

CONTENTS

INTRODUCTION

This is a cookbook, and like every cookbook ever published it is going to try and help you cook better. I hope to do this by passing on pretty much everything I've learnt over the last 35 years of cooking, listening, tasting, eating and cooking some more.

Basically, this is a book about 'the getting of knowledge'. As it's got my name and ugly mug on the front, it's about your getting of my knowledge and me talking about how I came by that knowledge in the first place, in the hope that this will be so reassuring that it will make you brave and enthusiastic enough to try the secrets shared over the coming pages.

As Forrest Gump once so memorably said (I suspect about me), 'I'm not a smart man'. I suppose this is why I regularly find myself having 'baby step' insights into why the things I cook work in the kitchen, so some of these secrets might seem obvious. If they do seem obvious, well, then you are already on your way to better cooking. Nice work!

I disagree that the devil is in the detail. For me, the detail of these baby steps is where the angels reside. These secrets to doing the little things better are all part of that elusive quest to master the dishes that we love to cook, love to share and, even occasionally, love to show off with, whether it's roast pork with perfect crackling, a braise that has guests licking their lips and mopping their plates, or a gooey slab of chocolate decadence that is just so deceptively simple to make. So please don't dismiss the smaller details, just absorb them.

I was no childhood kitchen prodigy but I have slowly edged towards competence through meticulously recording the steps and secrets that make things better when I cook a dish. (Although legend has it that I did make my first baked Alaska at aged seven. And that's one of the proper kind you bake in the oven, mind, not one of those cheating restaurant versions where they just blowtorch the meringue. God it feels good to get that out without the usual catcalls from certain fellow judges.)

These secrets have come from the broadest of places – from eating at street-food stalls and at the best restaurants in the world; from fellow home cooks, from CWA matriarchs and occasionally from some of the best chefs in the world, whom I have been lucky enough to work with over the

years and spend hours discussing food and what makes it good. What I hope you'll find in the coming pages is that the most effective tips to nailing a dish are actually very simple and logical – they just need to be pointed out!

It could be something as direct as Marco Pierre White's wisdom on how to make sauces, Mario Batali or Antonio Carluccio's brilliant insights into how to improve your pastas, Rick Stein's simple tips to demystifying the art of cooking seafood, Kirsten Tibballs or Darren Purchese's brilliance with chocolate and pastry or Maggie Beer's genius when it comes to cooking fowl. Or it might be more oblique learnings from inspirational thinkers like René Redzepi, Massimo Bottura or Heston Blumenthal, who you can talk to and literally hear them flipping the switches to give you multiple light bulb moments.

Wisdom is not only held in the minds of the great chefs but also comes from 'lesser lights' who are no less bright when it comes to cooking great dishes – names you've probably never heard of like Melly Beilby, Jen Ryan, Judy Bennison, Lyla Hatfield, my mum, my grandmother, chef Joe and my own formidable food team of Marnie Rowe and Kate Quincerot. Their fingerprints are all over the secrets and recipes in this book, too.

The aim of this book is to align all of these wonderful cooks behind you to help you cook dishes that – like a terrine or perfect pastry – might have previously confounded you or that you secretly knew you could cook better. One by one we want to help you master them, because these secrets are the building blocks for better cooking.

Some of these cooking secrets are, however, so blindingly obvious that we often take them for granted and then risk overlooking them. Too often when I play CSI with my occasional cooking disasters it is these that are the root of the problem.

So, to start you off, here's my list of the 12 Simple Secrets to Better Cooking That Are So Blindingly Obvious We Are Sometimes Blind to Them:

1. **Read and follow the recipe.** If you want to cook something that looks like the picture, you have more chance if you follow the recipe accompanying it. Sure, a recipe can only ever be a guideline, but it's better trying to drive to Gympie with a map than with blind intuition.

2. **If you must substitute, think about what the role of the previous ingredient was**. For example, if you don't have lemon use vinegar instead (in savoury dishes) or another citrus in sweet dishes – but pull back on the sweetness, as the lemon would have brought more tartness. Remember Rule #1, however: following is safer than freestyling!

3. **Don't substitute in pastry and baking.** There is little latitude in pastry recipes if you want to the get the rise, texture or crust promised in the picture.

4. **Keep it simple. Always.** Every ingredient you add to a salad, pasta sauce or braise increases the risk of things getting out of balance. Think like an Italian when you cook (but without the stereotypical obsessions with football, cars, girls and mamma)

and just concentrate on putting true flavours on a plate. Think roast pork with tart, butter-fried apples; penne tossed in a pan with cherry tomatoes, bocconcini and finished with torn fresh basil and a pinch of salt; or even a boiled egg with Vegemite soldiers. Simple. Perfect.

5. **Use ingredients at room temperature.** Cooking is basically just adding heat to stuff, so steaming your veg from room rather than fridge temperature will mean less cooking time and a more even cook. Obviously there are a few exceptions, like chocolate fondant puddings, but these only prove the rule that you leave stuff in the fridge only if you want the middle underdone. That's one of the ways I get a great bark-like crust on my thinner rare steaks.

6. **Prep ahead; be organised.** These days I like to lay out all my ingredients in order of use before I start cooking, to make sure I have everything and to make sure I have *enough* of everything! If people call you 'anal' make them do the washing up and also make sure you ignore Rule #7.

7. **Clean as you go.** This doesn't just make you look like a kitchen star, it will also help you feel in control and see where you put down that bloody basil.

8. **Clean things properly.** Don't 'boy wash'; be meticulous, do the job properly and see these clean-down moments as time to re-centre yourself for the next task. Visualise what you will be doing next. Become the stove and _____

_____ (please insert various other Eastern philosophy cooking analogies here).

9. **Always preheat the oven or grill before using.**

10. **Check the temperature of your oven.** Ovens are notoriously fickle. Buy an oven thermometer to make sure that your oven is running at 180˚C when it says it is. More bakes have been ruined by oven variation than anything else, but if you know you oven runs 10˚C hot you can make your own adjustments when you cook.

11. **Measure things out rather than guess.** Obviously!

12. **Cook by weight not volume.** Weight is exact whereas volume can vary dramatically based on density. For example, a cup of packed brown sugar weighs significantly more than a straight cup of the stuff due to the air between the granules.

One final Simple Secret: armed with the right information, cooking well isn't hard. Yes, you CAN do it! So, let's cook!

Don't forget to upload pictures of your triumphs on Insta or Twitter tagged with @mattscravat so I can share your happiness and pride!

PERFECT SALAD

SALADS AREN'T JUST ABOUT LEAVES AND VEG

SIMPLE IS BEST

SECRET #1: It is far more elegant to make salads with just one or a couple of ingredients . . . think iceberg lettuce with a simple yoghurt and herb dressing, or a tomato salad dressed with thinly sliced shallots and vinaigrette.

DON'T DRESS YOUR SALAD TOO EARLY

SECRET #2: Dress your salads at the table to avoid them going soggy and to stop soft leaves turning slimy.

SALADS AREN'T JUST FOR SUMMER

SECRET #3: Think of adding salads to your menus throughout the year. I love salads made with winter veggies like fennel and blood orange; or from roasted ingredients, like pumpkin or root veg. A salad built around frozen peas or frozen corn kernels can be a ray of summer sunshine when combined with mint or with chilli and lime, respectively. Or they can be reassuringly wintry if you toss the corn with roasted hazelnuts and caramelised onion, or the peas with crisp lardons of bacon and a sherry vinegar dressing. Building a salad around canned pulses in the same way can also achieve excellent results.

SECRET #4: It's very 'on trend' to use both fruit and carbs in salads. It could be something as hardcore as a sweet soy sauce-dressed rojak salad of hard fruits or something less confronting, like the Tomato and Plum Salad on page 20. I also love using ancient grains and other carbs as the heart of a salad. These form a sort of canvas on which to throw crunchiness from nuts or veg; bursts of sweetness from sultanas, dates or roasted parsnip; creaminess from dairy; and also some acidity in the form of anything from pickled chunks of lemon flesh to just the zest and juice. Finally, add some saltiness, either from something cured, something piggy, from a dairy ingredient, or even just from flaked salt!

MATCH THE SALAD TO THE PROTEIN

SECRET #5: Always think about how the salad will work with the protein you are serving and vice versa. If that lamb shoulder you're cooking is rubbed with coriander and cumin seeds, then follow this Muslim Mediterranean theme through to the salad by using dates, fresh mint and perhaps a little orange blossom water in the dressing. Oh, and perhaps it's best if it's a couscous or a freekeh salad, rather than just a bowl of butter lettuce with sliced cucumber and tomatoes!

PICKLE RATHER THAN DRESS

SECRET #6: I'm not a huge fan of dousing my salads in litres of olive oil and waves of acidic dressing. I'd far rather squeeze over the juice of a lemon or orange and let something creamy, like labneh or feta, provide the mouthfeel we'd usually get from olive oil. Similarly, that acidity could also be added by pickling an element from the salad – perhaps the cucumber, the shallots or ribbons of carrot or cabbage.

MANY SALADS RATHER THAN ONE

SECRET #7: Rather than piling everything into one of those technicolour main course salads that are so loved by Americans, it is far more sophisticated to assemble a number of simpler salads from the same bundle of ingredients. So, think of serving a carrot salad, a tomato salad, a cucumber salad and then a plain bowl of leaves instead. My ubersalads are the only exception to this rule – but that's because every element has a logical spot in building contrast in terms of texture and flavour.

CONTRAST TASTE

SECRET #8: There are times when I want the salad to be the hero of the meal and these more complex salads require multiple ingredients to make them worthy of top billing. At these times I look at assembling complementary ingredients that provide a good range of saltiness, sourness, sweetness, savouriness and a little bitterness. This same rule applies with simpler salads too . . . think how prosciutto and melon dressed with a little squeeze of lemon juice works so well together! Salt, savoury, sweet and sour – they are all there!

CONTRAST TEXTURES

SECRET #9: For me, a great complex salad is an exciting adventure in terms of both taste AND texture. While complementary textures can work (think of the three-way creaminess of a mayonnaise-dressed potato salad with hardboiled eggs, for example), contrasting textures are far more exciting. Think of ways to add crunch or creaminess in many forms: diced raw celery, cucumber cubes, macadamia nuts, toasted seeds and parboiled cauliflower for crunch, and marinated feta, slow-cooked leeks (and those macadamias and cauliflower) for creaminess. And think of what joy adding chewiness (from sultanas or candied carrots), or even crispiness (from fried shallots or croutons) might add.

LETTUCE SALADS SHOULD ALWAYS BE SIMPLE

SECRET #10: Nuff said. Plus lettuce salads should never include red oak or coral, both of which are evil.

PERFECT SALAD (CONTINUED)

What really lifts a good salad above the ordinary is a brilliant dressing, the likes of which you'll find over the next couple of pages. Me, I can't go past the best-ever instant mayo, taught to me by UK MasterChef winner Mat Follas. It debuted in my last book and was so good I thought it deserved a second outing, complete with a handy step-by-step guide …

INSTANT MAYO

1 egg
juice of ½ lemon
1 tablespoon Dijon mustard
salt flakes
300ml grapeseed oil

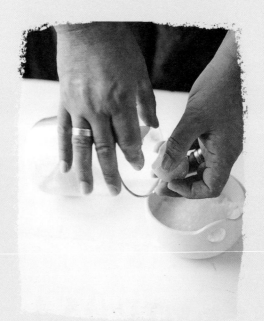

1. You'll need a stick blender to do this. Carefully crack the egg and place it in the base of the stick blender's plastic blending cup, without breaking the yolk.

2. Add the lemon juice.

3. Add the mustard.

4. Add a pinch of salt.

6. Place the stick blender in the blending cup and carefully position the head of the stick blender so it covers and encloses the egg yolk.

8. So, there's instant mayonnaise with no need for slow and tedious dribbling – of olive oil that is.

5. Pour over the grapeseed oil.

7. Press go and watch the head of the blender. Count to three and white ribbons should start to appear in the oil. Very slowly, pull the blender up through the oil and – voila! – the oil will emulsify with the egg and the lemon juice.

AN AVERAGE SALAD THAT BRINGS THE SWEETEST MEMORIES

Serves 4 for lunch
or 6 as a side

This is the salad my grandmother made for me when, as a small child, I stayed summer nights at her bungalow in the woods. She wasn't a great cook, but she was the first of our clan to buy fancy Dutch, whole-egg mayonnaise, rather than sweet and vinegary salad cream. It seemed oh so very sophisticated to a seven-year-old boy and it started a love affair with the creaminess of mayonnaise that still lingers through these pages. It's also the perfect first recipe for this book because it's about doing simple things better – and ideally doing them more simply too – whether it's a boiled egg or a homemade mayo. You'll only need about a cup of the mayo, but you can refrigerate the rest for another dish.

9 eggs, ideally at room temperature
4 baby cos lettuces, quartered
200 g good artisan cheese
  (see the NOTE below)

MAYO
1 egg
1 lemon
½ teaspoon English mustard
salt flakes
300 ml grapeseed oil

Place the eggs snugly in a saucepan with a lid. Cover with cold water, put on the lid and place on the heat. Bring to the boil and then remove from the heat. After 7 minutes, peel one of the eggs and check that the yolk is almost set. If it is, douse the other eggs in cold water to stop them cooking, then peel them too; you may find buttering your thumbs will make this easier. If the yolk is still a bit runny, then leave them in the water for 1 minute more.

Make the mayo (a slight tweak on the Instant Mayo on the previous page) using a stick blender with the normal double-ended blade. First, carefully crack the egg into the bottom of the transparent plastic or glass blending cup that fits the stick blender well. Then add the juice of half the lemon, the mustard and a good pinch of salt. Top with the grapeseed oil. Carefully sink the stick blender right down to the bottom of the container so that the metal safety basket/ cover that surrounds the blades covers and encloses the egg. Blitz, counting to three, or until you can see white ribbons forming at the bottom. When you do, slowly draw the stick blender up through the oil, which will blend it into the emulsifying white mass and turn it into mayonnaise. Taste and adjust the mayo with a little more salt or lemon juice.

Now it is time to plate. Instead of using a salad bowl, these days I like to spread things across a large platter. Start with the cos pieces, equally spaced, and intersperse with halves of the hardboiled eggs. Dollop the mayo artfully over the lettuce and eggs. Grate the cheese over everything and serve.

NOTE: *In a perfect world, use a combination of a great cloth-wrapped cheddar, like Ashgrove, with a Double Gloucester. Failing that, use a mixture of any red cheese and any good tasty. As a last resort, ordinary Cracker Barrel will have to do.*

PERFECT SALAD

GRILLED CUCUMBERS, COTTAGE CHEESE AND DILL

Serves 4 for lunch or a light supper

It's strange how a trip devoted to eating in three countries over eight days can be summed up in one superbly simple dish. For me, this combo encapsulates so much of what was cool about eating in Scandinavia: burning stuff – especially cucumbers and dairy products – and dill! Sure, there isn't any fermentation going on in this dish, and it would help if you foraged the cucumbers from the wild, but that cottage cheese does give a suggestion of lactic fermentation … sort of!

2 × 250 g packs of baby cucumbers (about 12)
½ lemon
1 × 250 g tub of cottage cheese (a salty, creamy, lumpy type like the Dairy Farmers one)
1 small bunch of dill

Preheat your grill or barbecue.

Roll the cucumbers around on the heat, cooking them like you would sausages. You want them to soften, blister and blacken in places, and turn from a bright green to a more muted olive colour.

At the same time, char the lemon half by placing it face down on the grill.

Once the cucumbers are charred, slice them lengthways into quarters. Arrange them in a rough lattice in a wide shallow bowl or along a long platter.

Dollop the cottage cheese into the natural gaps between the cucumber slivers.

Tear off the fronds of the dill and sprinkle them all over the cucumbers. Squeeze on the charred lemon and serve as a light meal or a tasty side for barbecued lamb or roasted salmon.

ASIAN KILLER SLAW

Serves 6 as a side

As it's so textural, slaw is a brilliant way of persuading kids and recalcitrant adults to eat veg – whether it's dressed with a punchy Thai dressing, like this one, or doused with a Japanese rice wine vinegar mayonnaise. The latter is great if you want something creamy in a wrap or on your plate, and if going the mayo way for kids – or less adventurous adults – think about dumping the herbs!

¼ red cabbage
¼ wombok
3 small red Asian shallots
1 carrot
handful of mint leaves, torn
handful of Thai basil leaves
handful of coriander leaves
handful of sugar snap peas,
   finely sliced lengthways
2 tablespoons chopped unsalted
   roasted peanuts, to serve

DRESSING
50 g (⅓ cup) unsalted
   roasted peanuts
2 teaspoons chilli flakes
4 tablespoons caster sugar
5 tablespoons lemon juice
3 tablespoons fish sauce

First shred or slice all the veg as finely as you can. If you don't already own a mandoline, use this salad as an excuse to buy one. Not only is it quicker and makes any slaw much easier, but it also makes it look as if you have brilliant knife skills. Make sure you always pre-cut the chunks of cabbage to fit the width of the mandolin. And use the guard, as sliced fingertips are not welcome in any slaw, no matter how 'killer' it is!

Next, make the dressing. Pound the peanuts using a mortar and pestle, then add the chilli flakes, sugar, lemon juice and fish sauce and stir until the sugar dissolves. If you don't already own a mortar and pestle – and don't need another excuse to shop – use the blunt end of a rolling pin in a small, high-sided, plastic bowl or pulse with your stick blender to roughly blend the dressing.

To make the salad, just combine all the salad ingredients, except for the peanuts, in a bowl. Pour over the dressing just before serving and toss, then scatter on the chopped peanuts and serve.

This is a perfect side for beef, chook or any South-East Asian curry or crispy fried naughtiness, like salt and pepper squid or crunchy soft-shell crab.

SNOW PEA MATCHSTICKS, SOYBEAN AND SESAME SALAD THAT ONCE WAS ALI'S*

Serves 4 as a light lunch

This beautiful salad makes a perfect light lunch and works wonderfully as a simple side with anything from steamed fish to thinly sliced beef fillet. To bulk it up, think of adding cold soba noodles, very finely sliced strips of daikon (fresh or lightly pickled), thin strips of just-poached chicken breast – or any combination of the three.

400 g snow peas, trimmed of any stalks
    and de-stringed
400 g soybeans in pods (sold in Asian
    grocery stores as frozen edamame)
2 tablespoons sesame seeds (black,
    white or a mixture)

DRESSING
1 tablespoon sesame oil
2 tablespoons mirin
1 tablespoon rice wine vinegar
1 teaspoon caster sugar
juice of 1 lemon, or to taste
1 teaspoon soy sauce, or to taste

Prepare a large bowl of iced water. The water is cold enough when ice you add to it doesn't melt.

Bring a pan of water to the boil and then reduce to a simmer. Working in small batches, plunge the snow peas into the water, count to 5, then use a slotted spoon to lift them straight into the iced water. Repeat until all the snow peas are very lightly blanched. They should be a lovely bright green. Once they are cold, you should drain them. Then pat them dry.

Put the pan of water back on the heat and return it to the boil.

Next, make the salad dressing by mixing together the sesame oil, mirin, rice wine vinegar and sugar. Add the lemon juice and soy sauce to taste. You want to add complexity to the acidity and you want some brightness from the lemon and salt from the soy, but don't let either dominate the sesame-mirin-vinegar combo. It's an intense dressing so you'll use it sparingly.

Plunge the soybeans into the boiling water and cook for 5 minutes, or until the beans are just cooked. Test one to make sure. Plunge the soybeans into the iced water to stop them cooking.

While the soybeans are chilling, slice the snow peas into matchsticks. Pod the soybeans directly onto a serving plate, then scatter on the snow pea matchsticks. Dress the plate with a little of the dressing but don't drown the greens. Sprinkle on the sesame seeds and serve with the extra dressing on the side.

I begged this salad off a friend and 'Ali's Snow Pea and Sesame Salad' was written at the top of the photocopied page ... hence the name.

TOMATO
AND PLUM
SALAD

Serves 4 as a side

Last year I snuck off to Stockholm with the woman I love to swing hands in one of the prettiest, hippest, but also most expensive, cities in the world. However, it was one of the cheapest meals – at uberchef Petter Nilsson's cool little restaurant at the Spiritmuseum – that provided the most culinary inspiration, including an unusual salad of plums and tomatoes which I've been making ever since. The secret here is that the acidity of the vinaigrette acts as a bridge between these two unlikely bedfellows, and the ricotta adds a creaminess loved by both. Try it!

8 heirloom or black russian tomatoes
3 plums
100 g ricotta, crumbled
basil leaves (or, failing that,
** chervil leaves)**

DRESSING
1 tablespoon red wine vinegar
½ teaspoon salt flakes
3 tablespoons extra-virgin olive oil
pinch of ground white pepper

Make the dressing by combining all the ingredients.

Cut the tomatoes into irregular shapes.

Slice the cheeks off the plums, then cut them into wedges.

Toss the tomatoes and plums in the dressing then pile them into a bowl or onto a platter. Scatter on the ricotta and nestle in the basil leaves. Serve immediately.

BRIAR SALAD OF BEETROOT, BLACKBERRY AND CELERY

Serves 6–8

I keep coming back to memories of blackberrying with my grandmother. It must have something to do with that earliest of associations: that you must go through pain to earn pleasure. In this case the clawing of the thorns led to the sweetest burst of juice from the blackberries. This dish actually began life as a dessert of blackberries with celery leaves, as they add a lovely green 'briar-ness', but without the danger of getting jabbed by thorns. When beetroot came knocking, though, it was easy to see how they'd all get along, especially with balsamic pushing the dish more firmly into the savoury world. It does still seem to vacillate a little between the two – but then that's the modern way, isn't it? Sweets veer more towards savouriness and savoury stuff is sweeter!!

4 beetroots
2 small celery stalks, plus the pale leaves from the centre of the bunch
1 tablespoon balsamic vinegar
1 tablespoon caster sugar
125 g blackberries
125 g (½ cup) crème fraîche

Preheat the oven to 180°C.

Wrap each beetroot individually in foil and bake in the oven for an hour.

Let the beetroots cool and then, using the foil and some paper towel, rub off the skins. Cut the beetroots into uneven purple wedges that might remind you of the sails of the Sydney Opera House, or shark fins, or even chunks of beetroot.

De-string the celery stalks, then cut them into small dice and reserve them in iced water.

In your smallest pan, heat the balsamic with the sugar to make an oozy syrup. Don't let it bubble away too much or else you'll get balsamic toffee, which can be stretched like taffy to decorate the finished dish. (Yeah, I did that the second time I made this salad, and it was rather fun if you have a silicon sheet that you can use to pull and push the toffee thin without burning your fingers!)

Cut one-third of the blackberries into halves – only the firmest mind you – so they look lovely and shimmery .

Spread the crème fraîche around a serving platter like a frame. Drain the diced celery and sprinkle it all over the inside of the frame. Arrange the beetroot chunks on top and then drop the whole blackberries around the chunks. Place the prettier blackberry halves in key positions. See above! Finally, tuck in around 20 little sprays of celery leaf, to add a pretty tonal change against all that purple, and to add a lovely 'briary' flavour.

Serve the salad with the balsamic syrup on the side … or drizzle it on at the table if you are a control freak! Just don't do it any earlier or it will encourage the beetroot to bleed into the crème fraîche in a rather macabre fashion.

THE 12 SIMPLE SECRETS TO THE

PERFECT UBERSALAD

The key secret to the perfect ubersalad is to always pick the sexiest ingredients – and what could be sexier than using SUPERFOODS?!* But not just any superfoods …

Nowadays the talk is all about kale and coconut oil, or cacao and chia seeds. But I say forget the chia-goji-amaranth salad with an almond-turmeric-linseed dressing and look at the more mundane SECRET superfoods (SSFs) that you've already got in your kitchen to build your own ubersalads worthy for inclusion in this book.

* Just one word about superfoods: always take them, or any claims about them, with a large pinch of salt!

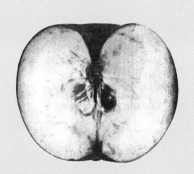

BEETROOT

SSF #3: Beetroot's purple colour is linked to the presence of antioxidants, and fans claim it offers protection from artery disease and that it lowers cholesterol. Roast it to serve at the heart of a salad with orange, hazelnuts or walnuts and goat's cheese, or with blackberries as on page 23. Or pickle shreds of beetroot to add brightness and tang to any grain salad.

APPLES

SSF #1: Apples keep the doctor away, or so goes the proverb, but little did our ancestors know that these crunchy health bombs are loaded with vitamin C and vitamin B, in all its glorious forms. Just remember to eat the skin, as that's where most of the goodness is. I love to cut an apple into batons and toss them into an iceberg lettuce and ricotta salad to add crunch and tang.

AVOCADOS

SSF #2: Avocados are a jolly good source of lutein as well as other carotenoids that are good for the eyes, and which are also supposed to help you extract more nutrition from the food you eat, according to a US study into National Health and Nutrition (2001–2008) published in the *Nutrition Journal*. The texture and flavour of avocados makes them perfect partners in salads, with everything from chicken and bacon to prawns. In any of these salad situations, pair them with lime juice, spring onions, roasted corn, cumin, finely diced chilli and coriander leaves to give a little Mexican flair to your ubersalad!

BLUEBERRIES

SSF #4: Blueberries are the flag-bearer of antioxidant fruits with a reputation for hunting and killing more potentially cancer-causing free radicals than any other fruit – although it's worth noting that wild blueberries have 48 per cent more antioxidants than farmed berries. Dried or fresh blueberries can add a pop of sweetness to any grain-based ubersalad.

BROCCOLI

SSF #5: Broccoli, according to my chums over at Body+Soul, offers some of the 'Most potent anti-cancer and anti-viral properties of any food'. Steam it lightly and then toss it through any grain salad along with loads of salty elements that work wonderfully with this veg's slight bitter notes. Think anchovies, capers or crispy pancetta.

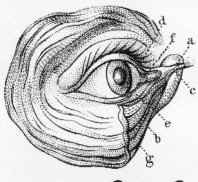

CARROTS

SSF #6: Carrots are loaded with beta-carotene which the body converts into vitamin A. This is good for eye health, amongst other things. I love slow-cooking carrots with honey or coriander seeds, or roasting them so they go all gnarly and extra-sweet, to form the base of a roast carrot salad. Otherwise I'll just cure carrot ribbons in sugar and salt to add crunch to any salad, or shred a couple of them to turn into a coleslaw or, after giving them a little burst in the microwave, as a softer 'hot slaw'. I never put grated carrot in any salad, uber or otherwise, because the rough surface that comes from grating is jarring to my finely tuned palate. Oh, and more importantly, it's just yuck!

CHILLI

SSF #7: Chilli is another food rich in beta carotene, but it also has seven times the vitamin C of an orange. Use chillies for crunch as well as for heat in cool salads, roast them to a softness to toss through grain salads or just blitz long red chillies with a little vinegar and salt to make a simple but vibrant condiment for your salad that will also fire up your digestion.

CITRUS

SSF #8: Citrus is almost mandatory in ubersalads and while I'd usually reach for the orange, lemon or lime, the grapefruit has attractions all of its own. Grapefruit, like so many other sour citrus fruits, may help fire up the digestion. I'd use grapefruit flesh for its sharpness and texture in Thai- or Mexican-inspired salads. Also try it as a little salad on its own with smoked salmon.

SALMON

SSF #9: Salmon is one of those oily fish, along with sardines and mackerel, which came to prominence over a decade ago, when nutritionists starting praising its high levels of polyunsaturated fats and omega 3, which is essential for protecting the heart, joints and cells. Add it smoked to a mayo-dressed potato salad along with some red onion dice, capers and fresh dill to turn it 'uber', or flake it hot smoked or panfried through any salad to add creaminess, richness and a salty burst.

SWEET POTATO

SSF #10: Sweet potato is another of those veg whose bright colour gives away its beneficially high levels of beta-carotene. Sweet potatoes are brilliant roasted in their skins because they go all fudgy and sweet, which is ace in any salad served with roast chook or pork.

TOMATOES

SSF #11: Tomatoes are one of the most potent goodness givers of all. As they come into full season, you need do no more than eat super-ripe tomatoes, sliced and mushed with stale bread, basil leaves, olive oil and a little flaked salt. Or serve a simple sliced tomato salad, covered with any soft herb, thinly sliced red onion, a fine grating of lemon zest and a fresh white cheese (such as good marinated feta, goat's curd or milky bocconcini or a mix of any of these). When using tomatoes in ubersalads be aware that their succulence can make other ingredients soggy – especially if you leave in the seeds. Better to remove the seeds and use them in the salad's dressing as they have bags of flavour.

YOGHURT

SSF #12: Yoghurt is good for the gut if you choose one that's loaded with live cultures. Yoghurt is great whether you are hanging it to make labneh to dollop on your ubersalad, tossing it with cumin, salt and cucumber to make the dressing, or just dunking chook pieces in it before dredging them with breadcrumbs to make the schnitzel pieces for that barley, corn, almond, spring onion, green capsicum and schnitzel ubersalad you've just invented. A Kewpie and maple syrup dressing would be great for this!

SHREDDED CHICKEN, BROWN RICE AND CORN WITH MISO DRESSING

Serves 6

I have been trying really hard to break free from my slavish devotion to bacon. OK, I admit it was an obsession that was everywhere in my last few books, and it was compounded by the pleasure I got from curing my own pancetta and guanciale.

However, I've now come to terms with the fact that I love smokiness and salt as much as the porkiness; so if I add those first two elements to a dish I can kick this addiction. In this recipe, smoked almonds play the role of the bacon, as whenever corn, chook and cashews get together something salty and smoky is needed too! It's a bit like the way you can't have a *Sesame Street* reunion without Elmo, as he adds the edge that Big Bird is missing. Miso in the dressing also brings a dirty umami hit and even more salty flavour – think Oscar the Grouch maybe?

200 g (1 cup) brown rice, cooked as
  per packet instructions
2 celery stalks, very finely diced
3 spring onions, very finely sliced into
  little coins
2 cooked sweetcorn cobs, kernels sliced
  off and reserved
80 g (½ cup) smoked almonds
1 supermarket roast chook, meat
  shredded

MISO DRESSING
115 g (¾ cup) unsalted cashews
1 tablespoon miso paste,
  preferably white
squeeze of lemon, to taste
pinch of salt flakes

To make the dressing, blitz the cashews in a food processor with the miso, lemon juice, salt and 120 ml of warm water to loosen it all up. The dressing should be creamy but pourable, and not a thick paste. Add a little more warm water if needed.

Toss the cooked brown rice with two-thirds of the celery, spring onion, corn and almonds and set the rest aside for later. (And it's OK, that can be *roughly* two-thirds as I don't want you wasting your time counting out sweetcorn kernels to divide by 66.66% recurring.) Mound into a wide shallow bowl or platter.

Toss the shredded chicken in the miso dressing and scatter on top of the rice. Sprinkle on the reserved celery, spring onion, corn and almonds and serve.

TIP: *Virtue tells us not to eat the chicken skin, but do think about tearing it up and throwing it over the salad as well. Yum! (Albeit a slightly guilty yum.)*

ZUCCHINI BURRATA

Serves 4 as a starter

On the surface of it, this is such an Italian dish, but I realised when we were photographing it that it was actually inspired by my trips to Scandinavia over the last few years. There they love to pair milkiness with the freshness of cucumbers and dill (witness the salad on page 14), and they have an almost obsessive compulsion with tinting that milkiness with green herb purées or oils. This visual deliciousness can be found all through René Redzepi's first *Noma* cookbook – in his fresh mackerel with grilled cucumber, his snowy squid with green strawberry granita and verbena parsley oil and in the cream and dill oil he serves with raw shrimp.

Realising this, it seems a bit weird that a simple home cook could be inspired by one of the best restaurants in the world – even for a dish as simple as this. But as we always say, respect where respect is due. So let this dish be your springboard to playing with the herbaceous flavours of green herbs and discovering how they partner with dairy's soft, mellow creaminess.

4–5 zucchini
juice of 1 lemon
pinch of salt flakes
200 g crème fraîche
1 burrata
2 tablespoons flaked almonds
freshly ground black pepper

BASIL OIL
200 ml good-quality extra-virgin
  olive oil
1 teaspoon salt flakes
1 bunch of basil (12 small leaves
  reserved for garnish)

To make the basil oil, use a food processor or stick blender to whiz the oil and salt together for about a minute, until just frothy. Doing this first helps stop the basil from discolouring when you add it. Add the basil leaves and whiz them in until you have a bright green sludgy oil.

Using a vegetable peeler, slice the zucchini lengthways into long flat ribbons. I like to keep the dark skin on the ribbons' edge. To do this, only take several layers off each side. You will be left with the inner white flesh/seeds to use for some other dish.

Divide the zucchini ribbons into two mounds. Place half of the zucchini ribbons in a snaplock bag with the lemon juice and a good pinch of salt. Leave for 15 minutes or longer to gently pickle.

Place the other half of the zucchini ribbons in a bowl of heavily iced water. Once they are cold (and you're ready to use them), drain and gently pat dry.

Spread the crème fraîche around the front third of a large serving platter or bowl, making sure NOT to smooth it out. You want lots of gullies and troughs in which the basil oil can pool. Place the burrata in the middle of the plate, with its belly just nestling into the crème fraiche.

Drain the pickling zucchini ribbons (save the lemony liquid from the snaplock bag) and mix them together with the iced ribbons. Arrange them around the back of the burrata in a crescent-shaped mound like a halo, or the fur collar of Jon Snow's cape. It's OK if the front edges of the zucchini touch the crème fraîche.

Drizzle the basil oil in the gullies and troughs of the crème fraiche, sprinkle over the flaked almonds, grind over some black pepper and serve.

Cut open the burrata and let your guests feast upon the ribbons of zucchini dressed with all that herby creaminess. Using the reserved salty lemon juice as seasoning is a good way to cut through some of that creaminess.

COCONUT POACHED-CHICKEN NOODLE SALAD

Serves 4 as a starter or 2 as a main

Coconut-poached chicken and noodle salad is one of the things that sustains us during the filming of *MasterChef*. It's the combination of the soft flavour of coconut milk with the verdant herbs and the brilliant green notes of the lime that make this dish so special.

DRESSING
140 ml coconut milk
2 tablespoons grated palm sugar
1 tablespoon fish sauce
1 ½ tablespoons lime juice
1 teaspoon grated ginger
1 garlic clove, finely chopped

SALTED CHILLI TOFFEE
170 g (¾ cup) caster sugar
½ teaspoon chilli flakes
120 g (¾ cup) unsalted peanuts, chopped
½ teaspoon salt flakes

COCONUT-POACHED CHICKEN
1 x 400 ml can coconut milk
2 kaffir lime leaves
1 slice of galangal or ginger
1 lemongrass stalk, bruised
1 red bullet chilli, split
½ teaspoon salt flakes
2 chicken breast fillets

SALAD
1 × 200 g packet thin rice stick noodles
¼ bunch of Thai or purple basil (or both if you can find them), leaves picked

¼ bunch of coriander, leaves picked
¼ bunch of mint, leaves picked
¼ bunch of Vietnamese mint, leaves picked
3 Lebanese cucumbers, peeled, halved, seeds removed with a teaspoon, finely sliced
2 red bullet chillies, deseeded, pith removed, finely sliced (optional)
1 drinking coconut (see TIP below)

Combine the dressing ingredients in a saucepan over low–medium heat. Simmer gently for 5 minutes. Set aside and leave to cool to room temperature. Just before serving, taste and adjust the dressing for balance. You want the flavour to be mellow and slightly savoury, so adjust to pull back any flavours that are too dominant, like the saltiness of the fish sauce or the brightness of the lime. You know the drill: if it's too sweet, address with more lime juice; if it starts to taste too much like an ice cream mix, add a couple more drops of fish sauce.

To make the salted chilli toffee, first pop a baking tray in the freezer to chill for 20 minutes. In a saucepan over low heat, add the caster sugar along with 2 tablespoons of water. Allow the sugar to dissolve completely, then increase the heat to a simmer and continue cooking until the caramel starts to turn golden and the bubbles slow down. Remove from the heat and stir in the chilli flakes (add more if you want it really spicy), peanuts and salt. Line the chilled tray with baking paper. Pour the salted chilli toffee onto the tray and spread it out into a thin layer. Set aside to harden, then chop it into a chunky crumble.

For the poached chicken, combine the poaching ingredients in a small saucepan that will hold the chicken breasts snugly. Bring to a gentle boil, then lower the heat and simmer for a few minutes before adding the chicken breasts. Continue simmering for 6 minutes, or longer if

they are large. Remove the chicken from the poaching liquid and leave to cool before slicing.

Cook the rice stick noodles according to the packet instructions.

Grab yourself a big serving plate and arrange the chicken, noodles, herbs, cucumber and chilli (if using) in separate bundles. Pour a little dressing over the chicken (serve the rest on the side), pile the young coconut flesh on top and sprinkle over the crushed toffee peanuts.

To eat, take a bit of everything onto your plate, pour on some of the extra dressing and gently toss all the ingredients together.

TIP: *Either ask your fruiterer to lop the top off your coconut or use a special coconut opener (these are becoming increasingly available in supermarkets). Use a long-handled teaspoon or dessertspoon to scoop out the flesh.*

TIP: *This dish is great garnished with fried rice-paper wafers. To make these, cut the dry rice paper into strips with scissors and fry them in a shallow pan with 2.5 cm very hot neutral oil. The rice paper strips will only take a second or so to puff up. Remove with a slotted spoon and sprinkle with a light dusting of roasted and ground Sichuan pepper mixed with salt.*

CARROT AND BAHARAT FENNEL 'STEAKS' WITH SAFFRON LABNEH

Serves 6

Like a marriage, this dish can be hot (as roast veg with garnishes) or cold (as a salad). Feel free to add lamb and dates, or roast chicken or even a pork fillet. You'll need to make the labneh the night before.

olive oil
1 kg carrots
1 teaspoon salt flakes
1 tablespoon caster sugar
2 large fennel bulbs, base and tops
   neatly trimmed, nicest fronds reserved
90 g (¾ cup) almond slivers
juice of 1 lemon
1 tablespoon honey

1 tablespoon coriander seeds, toasted
   and crushed
250 ml (1 cup) young muscat (or failing
   that, sweet sherry)
½ bunch of mint, leaves picked

SAFFRON LABNEH
250 g (1 cup) Greek yoghurt
8 drops of rosewater
¼ g saffron (½ a little supermarket tub)

**ORANGE–BAHARAT
SPICE MIX**
1 teaspoon ground cumin
1 teaspoon ground coriander
1 teaspoon ground cinnamon
1 teaspoon ground cloves
½ teaspoon freshly grated nutmeg
zest of ½ orange
½ teaspoon sugar
½ teaspoon salt flakes

To make the labneh, line a sieve with a double layer of new Chux or a piece of clean muslin and sit it over a bowl. Dollop in a third of the yoghurt and top with 4 drops of rosewater and half the saffron threads. Repeat. Finally, dollop in the rest of the yoghurt, gather up the edges of the cloth and secure with an elastic band. Place the bowl, sieve and balled yoghurt in the fridge overnight for the whey to leach out. Keep it wrapped in the cloth until needed.

The next day, start at least 2 hours before you want to eat. Preheat the oven to 180°C. Squirt some oil into a baking dish and roll all the carrots, bar one, around in it. When the carrots feel soft they are perfect. This can take anywhere from 40–80 minutes.

Take the remaining carrot and peel it into the widest, longest possible ribbons. Mix the salt and sugar in a snaplock bag or small dish. Put the carrot ribbons in and toss them around well. Set them aside to cure.

To make your orange–baharat spice mix, dry toast the spices over high heat for a minute or two until fragrant. Remove from the heat and toss in the orange zest. Move it around the pan to dry out for another couple of minutes. Tip onto paper towel and cool.

Remove the coarse outer petals of each fennel bulb (keep them for making stock). Slice off the rounded 'cheeks' on each wide side of each bulb and keep these 4 little cheeks and the fennel fronds. Cut each bulb, from top to base, into 3 × 1 cm fennel 'steaks'. Lay them on a shallow, oiled baking tray, drizzle with more oil and place in the oven.

Make sure you flip them over at the 20-minute mark or when they are tanned on the pan side. Then sprinkle over a dusting of the baharat spice mix. (Reserve the rest of the baharat for later use.) Continue cooking the fennel steaks for 20–30 minutes. They'll be done when both sides are golden and the flesh is soft.

Toast the almond slivers in the oven on a baking tray. You may need to give them a toss to ensure even colouring. Watch them and don't let them burn. Once they start to turn they will brown quickly. When toasted spread out on baking paper to cool and crisp up. Cut the reserved fennel cheeks into small dice, put them in a small bowl and cover with a good squeeze of lemon juice and a glug of olive oil.

When the carrots are ready, take them out of the oven, cut them in half lengthways and drizzle their cut faces with the honey and the coriander seeds. Give them another 10 minutes in the oven, so the honey can melt in, then lift them onto a warm plate and keep them warm. Deglaze the pan with the muscat and cook until it becomes syrupy.

Now it's time to serve, so rinse the carrot ribbons and pat them very dry. Arrange the 6 roasted fennel steaks on a large serving board and tumble the carrots on and around them. Curl up the cured carrot ribbons and tuck them in, then sprinkle on the fennel dice. Dollop on small spoonfuls of saffron labneh and fill in any gaps with the mint leaves and fennel fronds. Finally, drizzle on the muscat syrup and sprinkle on the toasted almonds.

POTATO SALAD WITH CHICKEN, LEEK AND FRESH HERBS

Serves 6–8

Some salads are designed to be ubersalads, the sort of super-salad that's the salad equivalent of a one-tray bake or a one-pot braise – a complete main course in one dish. Others just grow into the role, masquerading as a salad until finally we realise that they need to be promoted to the ubersalad section. This is one such dish – it was just too hulkingly delicious to leave languishing among the other potato salad recipes, which surveys show are only ever searched for in the months of December and January. This dish is year-round deliciousness!

800 g small potatoes, washed and skins left on
120 ml extra-virgin olive oil
800 g chicken tenderloins (around 16)
salt flakes and freshly ground black pepper
zest of 1 lemon
2 large or 3 smaller leeks, mainly the white parts, washed
6–8 tarragon sprigs, leaves picked
½ bunch of chives, finely chopped

DRESSING
125 g (½ cup) crème fraîche
125 g (½ cup) yoghurt
zest and juice of ½ lemon
salt flakes and freshly ground black pepper, to taste
2 tablespoons fresh thyme leaves

Make the dressing by whisking all the ingredients together in a bowl. Set aside.

Place the whole potatoes in a saucepan of water, bring to the boil and simmer until they are tender. Once they are cooked, drain and set them aside to cool down a bit.

When the potatoes are just cool enough to handle, cut into halves or quarters and place in a large mixing bowl. Toss gently in half the dressing. The warm potatoes will suck the dressing up, which is why we are leaving the rest for later.

While the potatoes are cooking, heat 2 tablespoons of the oil in a frying or griddle pan and cook the chicken tenderloins for 2 minutes on each side. Season with salt and pepper and the lemon zest. Yes, you could also use a barbecue flatgrill and cook these a la plancha.

Cut the leeks into 6–7 cm pieces, then halve them lengthways and slice into long shreds. Heat another 4 tablespoons of oil in a large frying pan set over medium heat. Sauté the leeks with a pinch of salt until they are cooked and burny bits start to appear. You may have to turn up the heat to char, but stick by them so they don't go too far.

To serve, lay the dressed potatoes on a large serving platter and top with the chicken pieces. Drizzle on the remaining dressing, making sure some of it hits the chicken. Finish with a scattering of the fried leeks as well as the tarragon and chives.

VEGETARIAN ROAST PUMPKIN SORT-OF-SALAD, WITH OPTIONAL ROAST CHICKEN

Serves 6

I dreamt up this recipe – literally. I woke up one morning, after dreaming that I'd made a really delicious dish of baked pumpkin wedges with a turmeric vinaigrette. Because real life is better than dreams, this recipe is better too. And that's mainly because of a breakfast I had a few months later with my dream woman at my local cafe, Gardiner and Field. It was poached eggs served with a dish of roast pumpkin, paired with beetroot, hummus and feta. A lovely idea! To try their original version, head to leafy Armadale in Melbourne. To try mine, pop up in my dreams and ask me to make it for you – or try the recipe below. And vegetarians, just leave out the chook!

1 × 750 g butternut pumpkin
olive oil
1 teaspoon ground turmeric
1 teaspoon coriander seeds, crushed
zest and segments of 1 orange
1 × 220 g tub hummus
large handful of spinach leaves (80–100 g)
30 green olives (ideally Sicilian)
70 g (around ½ cup) pepitas

70 g (generous ½ cup) sunflower seeds
200 g feta (soft, marinated feta is best, or see TIP)
1 supermarket roast chook, meat and skin roughly torn (just like in the photo)
salt flakes

QUICKLED BEETROOT
140 g beetroots

½ teaspoon fine salt
2 teaspoons caster sugar
1 tablespoon vinegar (white wine or cider vinegar work best)

TURMERIC DRESSING
6 cm piece of turmeric (peeled)
200 g Greek yoghurt
½ teaspoon freshly ground black pepper
good-quality extra-virgin olive oil

Preheat the oven to 150°C. This is lower than usual, but we want the pumpkin to get crispy, golden and chewy – which is also why we slice the pumpkin into thin wedges.

Halve the pumpkin, scrape out the seeds and threads with a metal spoon and slice lengthways into thin wedges. You can leave the skin on – well, unless you have no teeth.

Using your largest baking tray, toss the pumpkin in a slosh of olive oil. Sprinkle on the turmeric, coriander seeds and half the orange zest. (You'll use the rest of the zest and the juice/flesh later.) Bake in the oven for an hour. Check and turn at 45 minutes.

While the pumpkin is turning into chewy pumpkin candy, prepare the 'quickled' – that's quick pickled – beetroot and the dressing. Using rubber gloves or judiciously positioned paper towel, peel and finely grate the the beetroot. Use a mandoline with a shredder blade or lie a box grater down on its side over a plate. Mix the grated beetroot with the salt and sugar. Leave for 15 minutes, then stir in the vinegar and place in the fridge.

To make the dressing, grate the fresh turmeric into the yoghurt then add the black pepper. Blitz with a stick blender to get a pretty yellow sauce. Tip this into a serving bowl and pour on 2 tablespoons of your best olive oil. Don't mix it in.

Cut the orange segments into thirds. Reserve these pieces and any juice.

When the pumpkin is golden and sticky, remove it from the baking tray. Spread the hummus over an attractive shallow serving bowl. Scatter on the spinach leaves and lay the chewy pumpkin wedges on top. Sprinkle on the olives and both lots of seeds.

Next, judiciously place little dollops of the feta and the quickled beetroot into any of the gaps or on top of any peaks in the bowl. Your eye will tell you where they need to fall.

To dress, draw your spoon through the turmeric dressing and then spoon a little over the salad so it pools in places, the oil marbling into the turmeric dressing. Sprinkle over the last of the orange zest, along with the orange pieces and any juice. Top with the roast chook, if you're so inclined, and finish with a sprinkle of salt flakes.

TIP: *Can't get marinated feta? Then make whipped feta instead. Check out my simple recipe on page 109.*

TIP: *I've added black pepper to the turmeric dressing because there is a body of thought that says it makes the nutritional benefits of turmeric easier to absorb – and it makes no difference to the recipe either way!*

PERFECT ANCIENT GRAINS SALAD

If food had gangs then the coolest gang in the neighbourhood at the moment would be the 'Ancient Grains'. They'd have leather jackets with their colours – probably a selection of earthy tones – and 'Ancient Grain MC' emblazoned on them. It would also be an eclectic group with very weird membership criteria, because although this gang is identified with being gluten free, many of the members aren't. And even the word 'grain' in the title is misleading, because members include both seeds and pseudograins, neither of which are grains at all.

WHO'S IN THE ANCIENT GRAINS GANG?

SECRET #1: Amaranth, barley, buckwheat, millet, quinoa, rice (brown, red, black and other colours except for evil white), rye, sorghum (aka milo), teff, wild rice and old varieties of wheat, such as spelt, emmer (aka farro), einkorn, freekeh and kamut. Linseed, sunflower seeds and chia seeds seem to have some sort of honorary membership of the Ancient Grains gang too.

WHICH ARE GLUTEN FREE?

SECRET #2: Amaranth, buckwheat, millet, quinoa, the rices, sorghum, wild rice, teff and other seeds are all gluten free. Barley, rye and the wheats aren't.

WHY DO WE CARE?

SECRET #3: It used to be that these grains were more hippy than a Grateful Dead concert in Nimbin, but when the veg-loving likes of the late US uberchef Charlie Trotter put them on their menus around the millennium, these grains became more than just something people from far-flung corners of the world ate in anthropological docos.

It's no wonder that these grains and seeds have become popular again in this food-as-health era as they are often high-protein, low-GI and some are even gluten free. Also many are whole grains and thus offer the nutritional benefits of bran, germ and endosperm of the kernel. They also offer culinary excitement in terms of both texture and taste – whether that's chewy and nutty or puffy and toasty.

HOW TO USE THEM

SECRET #4: These grains and seeds are remarkably versatile, although you need to be aware which maintain their structure (spelt, barley) and which can become gluggy (amaranth, quinoa). Remember, too, that many are used as soupy-type dishes in their countries of origin. For example, sorghum* is the go-to grain for breakfast porridge in parts of Africa. The simplest thing to do with these grains and seeds at home is to substitute them for rice as the gravy-soaking carb to go with braises and stews. But they also act well as the bulk in salads; just make sure those salads have loads of crunchy textures and sharp, bright, salty flavours to go with them – and make sure you don't overcook them.

* For the record, I think sorghum is overrated other than for porridge in Africa, or making beer from, or feeding animals.

HERE ARE MY SEVEN FAVOURITE ANCIENT GRAINS

QUINOA

#5: Quinoa is the popular one, a seed that's not only higher in protein than most grains but that also contains all of the essential amino acids, making it a rarity in the plant world. I love using quinoa in stuffings instead of couscous or breadcrumbs, in a pilaf instead of rice, to bulk up fishcakes and koftes, and in all manner of salads – both cooked with stock and fried. For perfect fluffy quinoa gently simmer 200 g (1 cup) of quinoa with 500 ml (2 cups) of stock or water for 12 minutes. Remove from the heat, cover and leave for 10 minutes to steam and fluff up.

MILLET

#1: Millet is the cool one in the gang, the grain most likely to become the next big thing. This ancient seed comes across like small couscous, but is far sexier. It is gluten free, rich in iron and B vitamins and quick to cook. I like to toast millet in butter before cooking it like quinoa.

FARRO

#3: Farro used to be known as 'emmer' wheat back when it was a staple for the Roman legions. It's still popular in Italy, where the flour is used to make pasta and the grains pop up in Tuscan soups. I reckon it's great with Mediterranean flavours and, if serving under grilled fish, I'll fry the stock-cooked grains with leeks in a little olive oil and butter, to give it an even tastier edge. Look for wholegrain or 'whole' farro that takes longer to cook (40+ minutes, rather than 15 for other, often pre-steamed, farros).

SPELT

#6: Spelt is a nutty Bronze Age wheat that's been grown since 5000 BCE. I treat the berries like barley and cook them in double the volume of stock until they soften, which can take from 30–60 minutes. If all the stock gets absorbed during the cooking, add extra water by the half cup. Spelt is one of my favourite ancient grains to use in salads, especially with creamy dressings, steamed cauliflower or good feta.

FREEKEH

#2: Freekeh is roasted green wheat from North Africa that is both high in fibre and low-GI. The roasting process gives it a slightly smoky flavour, which makes it interesting to use in pilafs and salads – especially with ingredients that echo or highlight that smokiness, like smoked almonds or smoked ricotta. Cook freekeh in loads of water, first bringing it to the boil and then simmering until done. Nibbed freekeh will take as little as 15 minutes, but has a tendency to go mushy, so I usually use the whole grain, which can take anything from 30–60 minutes, in the worst case scenario.

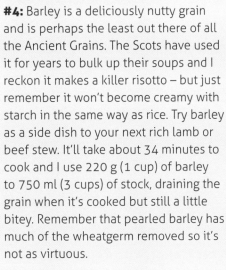

BARLEY

#4: Barley is a deliciously nutty grain and is perhaps the least out there of all the Ancient Grains. The Scots have used it for years to bulk up their soups and I reckon it makes a killer risotto – but just remember it won't become creamy with starch in the same way as rice. Try barley as a side dish to your next rich lamb or beef stew. It'll take about 34 minutes to cook and I use 220 g (1 cup) of barley to 750 ml (3 cups) of stock, draining the grain when it's cooked but still a little bitey. Remember that pearled barley has much of the wheatgerm removed so it's not as virtuous.

AMARANTH

#7: Amaranth is a tiny, nutritious seed that's high in iron, calcium, protein and amino acids like lysine. It is classified as a pseudocereal but, given its size, it needs to be cooked with care to stop it going gluggy. To avoid this, cover and let it steam at the end of cooking, as you do quinoa. You'll know it's done when it has tripled in size. Also, try popping it and mixing with melted sugar as a treat.

KALE, SWEET POTATO AND QUINOA SALAD

Serves 4

Where did it all go wrong? Turn your back for one moment, and suddenly dweebs, nerds and geeks are cool and the whole Bad Boy thing is on the nose. As it is at TV high schools with their pitch-perfect Glee Clubs, or post-school in Silicon Valley, so it is in the vegetable kingdom. Daggy old kale, sweet potato and that Peruvian kid are now the coolest things in class. Dress them in acidity and sweetness to balance kale's bitterness and add the fragrance of orange to bring that roasty-toasty sweet potato alive, and it's a makeover that'll convert even the toughest, hooded-bedroom-eyed, monosyllabic, leather-jacketed Bad Boy to believing that 'keen-wah' isn't quite so dull and worthy. Actually, it's kinda hot!

2 sweet potatoes (550–600 g), skin on, cut into 2 cm dice
3 ½ tablespoons extra-virgin olive oil
salt flakes and freshly ground black pepper
185 g (1 cup) cooked quinoa (see page 39)
1 bunch of kale, tough stalks removed, very finely sliced
70 g (½ cup) pepitas
50 g (around ⅓ cup) sunflower seeds
80 g (½ cup) smoked or roasted almonds

DRESSING
150 ml red wine vinegar
3 tablespoons soft brown sugar
75 g (½ cup) currants
zest and juice of ½ orange

Preheat the oven to 180ºC.

Toss the sweet potato in 2 tablespoons of the oil and season with salt and pepper. Bake for 25–30 minutes, or until cooked.

While the sweet potato is roasting, make the dressing. Combine the red wine vinegar and sugar in a saucepan set over low heat. Turn up the heat a little and simmer for a few minutes, then add the currants and simmer for a few minutes more. Add the orange zest and juice and remove from the heat. Set aside.

Toss the sweet potato, cooked quinoa and kale in a bowl together with half the dressing, and season with salt and pepper to taste.

Assemble the salad by piling it into a large shallow bowl or onto a platter. Sprinkle on the pepitas, sunflower seeds and almonds. Spoon over the remaining dressing and drizzle with the remaining extra-virgin olive oil.

If you want to add a bit of protein, this salad would be great with grilled lean chicken such as fillet or tenderloins.

CRISPY QUINOA WITH AVOCADO, TOMATO, LIME AND CHILLI

Serves 4

Allow me to let you into the greatest secret of this dish; the one thing that, when you understand it, will lift your cooking to a new level … In this dish I fry the quinoa to make it crispy. It's a great thing to do as it makes quinoa texturally far more exciting – and it ends up tasting better too! This is also a wonderful thing to do with cracked wheat. There's no space for that recipe here, but if you tweet me a photo of something you've cooked from this book, I'll tell you where I've hidden your free copy of this cracked wheat recipe and you can go and get it. But you'll need to ask for directions.

100 g (½ cup) quinoa, rinsed
vegetable oil
1 avocado, sliced
1 × 250 g punnet cherry tomatoes,
   chopped as you like
½ jalapeño chilli, deseeded, pith
   removed, finely diced
¼ bunch of coriander, leaves picked
salt flakes

DRESSING
2 limes, segmented and each segment
   cut into thirds
1 ½ tablespoons extra-virgin olive oil
½ teaspoon salt flakes

Gently simmer the rinsed quinoa in 250 ml (1 cup) of water for 12 minutes. Remove from the heat, cover and leave for 10 minutes to steam and fluff up.

Heat a splash of vegetable oil in a frying pan over medium heat. Spread the quinoa evenly in the pan and fry for 3–4 minutes. (You may need to do this in batches, depending on the size of your pan.) You want the quinoa to have contact with the hot, oiled metal of the pan so the moisture steams off and it can go toasty and crispy. So don't harass the quinoa in the pan; try not to stir it unless it looks like it is going to burn. After 3–4 minutes, give it a toss and leave it to brown for a few more minutes. Continue until the quinoa is all crunchy.

To make the dressing, mix the lime flesh with the olive oil and salt in a small bowl and set aside in a warm place for at least 15 minutes. This softens and mellows the stringent acidity of the lime flesh, so you can load more of the lime carpels onto the salad.

To serve the salad, combine the avocado, tomatoes and crunchy quinoa in a bowl or a large platter. Sprinkle over the jalapeño and coriander leaves, then pour on the lime and oil dressing and sprinkle with salt flakes to taste. Serve immediately.

SPELT SALAD WITH RAS EL HANOUT CARROTS, MINT, POMEGRANATE AND ORANGE FOR LUCY

Serves 2 or 4 as a side

I felt a bit funny writing this recipe, knowing that it was going to be edited by the woman who co-wrote the definitive book on Middle Eastern cuisine, *Arabesque*. I suppose the good thing is that since the recipe is still in the book, she must have approved of the Moroccan spice mix ratios and the overall deliciousness of the dish. Yay! Well done, me!

175 g (1 cup) spelt, well rinsed
500 ml (2 cups) chicken stock
1 tablespoon walnut oil
2 tablespoons pomegranate molasses
1 orange, peeled and pith removed,
  divided into segments
¼ red onion, finely chopped
seeds from ½ pomegranate
½ bunch of mint, leaves picked and torn
½ teaspoon salt flakes
½ teaspoon sumac

RAS EL HANOUT CARROTS
5 carrots, cut into smallish chunks
2 teaspoons ras el hanout spice mix
  (see TIP below)
½ teaspoon salt flakes
freshly ground black pepper
1 tablespoon honey
1 tablespoon extra-virgin olive oil

Put the spelt in a saucepan with the stock and 250 ml of water (the ratio should be 3 parts liquid to 1 part grain). If you're just using water, then add a few pinches of salt. I'm using a combo of stock and water because I'm indecisive. Bring to the boil over medium–high heat, then reduce the heat to low and simmer until the grain is tender. This generally takes about 50 minutes. Keep an eye on the pan and add more water if it gets a bit too dry. Once cooked, drain well, then tip into a mixing bowl and set aside to cool. You want the grain to still be a little nutty and definitely not soggy.

While the spelt is cooking, preheat the oven to 180°C.

Toss the carrot chunks in the ras el hanout, salt, pepper, honey and oil. Spread on a baking tray and roast in the oven for 30 minutes, or until cooked and coloured.

When you're ready to serve, toss the spelt with the walnut oil and pomegranate molasses. Cut the orange segments into small wedges and add them to the spelt with all the remaining ingredients, including the roasted carrots. Toss together gently, then tumble onto a platter and serve.

TIP: *To make your own proprietary ras el hanout – 'head of the household' – spice mix: toast separately, then grind together 1 teaspoon cumin seeds, 2 teaspoons coriander seeds, 2 blades of mace, seeds from 4 cardamom pods, 1 teaspoon black peppercorns, 1 teaspoon ground cinnamon and 1 teaspoon fennel seeds (or 1 teaspoon dried liquorice root, if you can find it). Use what you need for this recipe and save the rest to rub on lamb or chicken or to sprinkle over cauliflower or fennel while roasting.*

PERFECT POTATO SALAD

STEAM FOR FLAVOUR

SECRET #1: Steam small or new potatoes to maximise flavour rather than boiling them.

SIMMER DON'T BOIL

SECRET #2: If you insist on boiling your potatoes because 'that's what nanna always did', then salt the water rather well. Oh, and rather than boiling, simmer them! PS Dave Hughes, is that you in that pic up above?

CUT EVENLY

SECRET #3: If you are going to cut potatoes, then cut them all the same size to ensure even cooking.

CHOOSE THE RIGHT POTATO

SECRET #4: Waxy potatoes are generally best for creamy dressings, but a floury potato, tossed while still warm with a stock-based dressing, does have its own unique attraction.

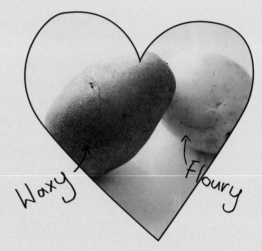

Waxy

Floury

KNOW WHEN TO PEEL

SECRET #5: If you must peel potatoes, do so after you cook them. That way the skins will flavour the water and they will just slip off when it comes time to peel. Far easier!

KNOW WHEN TO DRESS

SECRET #6: For stock- or vinaigrette-dressed potato salads, dress the potatoes while they are warm, so they soak up the dressing.

WHEN USING MAYO...

SECRET #7: For a mayo-dressed potato salad, as soon as the potatoes are tender, plunge them into iced water to arrest their cooking. Soggy, overcooked potatoes make for a poor creamy potato salad. Also, dressing hot potatoes will make your mayo oily; lukewarm is fine.

DRESS LIGHTLY

SECRET #8: A potato salad should be all about the potatoes, so don't use too much dressing, or a dressing that is too heavy. For this reason I never use straight mayo for a potato salad, but cut it with yoghurt, crème fraîche or lemon juice.

ADD SOME TANG

SECRET #9: The rather neutral flavour of potatoes means they love a little acidity. Try tossing them in a splash of vinegar while still warm, or use lemon juice, vinegar or yoghurt in your dressing. You can also add lightly pickled red onion, capers or gherkins – or even just a dash of the pickling juices from the jar.

CHECK SEASONING

SECRET #10: If you've kept your potato salad in the fridge, remember to adjust the seasoning before you serve it, as the saltiness will deceptively drop away when it is cold.

CRUNCH COMES LAST

SECRET #11: Only add crunchy elements (like nuts) or tender elements (like herbs) at the last moment (as you are about to eat) or they will soften in a most unwelcome manner.

CONTRAST TEXTURES

SECRET #12: Potatoes have a creamy texture, so if your dressing is creamy too, then add something for contrast. The crunch of celery, the sweet pop of toasted sweetcorn, the salty snap of crispy bacon and capsicum can all add a pleasing contrast in terms of both texture and flavour.

VINTAGE POTATO SALAD

Serves 6–8 as a side

I have long wondered what the difference is between second-hand clothes, op shop clothes and vintage. Then it came to me. The difference is only in terms of how much we have to pay. Second-hand items are about 35 per cent of the original retail price, op shop clothes are ten per cent (or less), while vintage, thanks to our friends the hipsters and the retro-fashionistas, are 100 per cent *higher* than the original price. You could buy something new for that, you know.

This salad is a perfect hipster's rebuff to that damaging and deluded claim – for this potato salad is a classic that will never go out of style! And it goes with everything – but especially with any lamb, any chicken, lobster, prawns, beef, pretty much anything from the barbecue, hardboiled eggs, quail, roast poussin, pork, poached or steamed fish or even just grouped with a whole load of other salads. It's like that perfect vintage leather jacket … just saying … but a whole lot cheaper!

1 kg potatoes (a waxy variety like
   kipfler, pink eye or nicola), peeled
   and quartered
125 g (½ cup) whole-egg mayonnaise
125 g (½ cup) sour cream
2 tablespoons apple cider vinegar
salt flakes and freshly ground
   black pepper
4 spring onions, finely sliced
6 gherkins, finely chopped
3 tablespoons chopped flat-leaf
   parsley leaves
¼ bunch of dill, chopped

Cook the potatoes in a large saucepan of boiling, salted water for 8–10 minutes, or until tender. Drain briefly, then throw them back into the warm, dry pan to steam dry and cool for 15 minutes.

Mix the mayonnaise with the sour cream and apple cider vinegar to make a dressing. Season to taste with salt and pepper.

Tip the potatoes into a large mixing bowl and toss them gently with half the spring onions and most of the gherkins, parsley and dill, leaving the rest for garnish.

Pour the dressing over the potatoes while they are still a little warm, so they soak up some of the flavours. Scatter the remaining ingredients on top as a garnish, take to the table and toss just before serving.

This potato salad is pretty much perfect with anything. Well, other than apple crumble, Armageddon or a Mariah Carey album!

POTATO SALAD WITH DOUBLE MINT

Serves 8 as a side

I have, over the years, pushed towards the total dissolution of the 'parliament of herbs' that sits in a draw near my stove. While I delight in my spices, with the exception of bay leaves and the occasional bit of dried Mexican oregano, dried herbs are dead to me. Then one day, Marnie (my muse) turned me on to dried mint, by selling it as something exotic and Middle Eastern.

I'm a sucker for the lure of exoticism – even if it only comes from the spice aisle of my neighbourhood supermarket. And by golly, when paired with the smoky souk-whiff of cumin, doesn't dried mint bring a sort of Ali Baba-meets-the-Arabian Knights (in diaphanous harem pants with some well-oiled and muscled eunuch on the side) raunch to the demure-Francophile-cottage garden vibe of this potato salad. It's very good and very, very great with lamb – but don't let this advice hamstring you! Just make the dried mint and cumin dressing at least a couple of hours (and preferably a day) ahead, so the flavours can infuse.

800 g small potatoes (a waxy variety like
  kipfler, pink eye or nicola), skins on
½ bunch of mint, leaves picked and torn
¼ bunch of flat-leaf parsley, leaves
  picked and torn

DOUBLE MINT DRESSING
2 teaspoons dried mint
½ teaspoon ground cumin
½ teaspoon salt flakes, plus extra
  to serve
½ lemon
1 × 200 g tub crème fraîche

For the dressing, stir the dried mint, cumin, salt and a squeeze of lemon into the crème fraîche and pop it into the fridge until you are ready to serve.

Cook the potatoes in a large saucepan of boiling, salted water for 8–10 minutes, or until tender. Drain briefly, then throw them back into the warm, dry pan to steam dry and cool for 15 minutes.

Cut the potatoes in half, quarters or discs, as you like (or leave them whole if they're really teeny). When the potatoes have cooled to room temperature, toss them gently with the dressing until nicely coated.

Scatter on the fresh herbs, finish with a sprinkle of salt and serve.

WARM SWEET POTATO SALAD WITH CONFIT SHALLOTS

Serves 2 as a main or
4 as a side

Before you send me an angry tweet, yes, I know that the sweet potato bears no botanical connection to the ordinary potato, however, it has to be said that it does work almost as well in a cold salad. And maybe it's even slightly better once roasting has turned it into something between a sweet vegetable version of taffy and fudge.

Apparently the sweet potato was Henry VIII's favourite vegetable, and we all know about his prodigious appetites! Here, it is reunited with a couple of fellow migrants from the Americas – maple syrup and pecan nuts. This is the sort of potato salad to make when you want something that's a little bit dirty, a little bit decadent and with just enough sourness to keep things interesting.

16 French shallots, skins on
250–350 ml extra-virgin olive oil
1 teaspoon salt flakes, plus extra
1 tablespoon good-quality red wine
   vinegar
1 large sweet potato (around 600 g),
   peeled and sliced 1–1.5 cm thick
freshly ground black pepper
8 slices streaky bacon
2 tablespoons maple syrup
2 tablespoons sultanas
40 g butter
squeeze of lemon juice
100 g (1 cup) pecans

Preheat the oven to 190°C.

Bring a large saucepan of water to the boil, drop in the shallots and blanch them for 1 minute. Tip the shallots into a colander to drain, then peel them, taking care to keep the root end on so they remain intact.

In a saucepan or high-sided frying pan, heat all but 2 tablespoons of the olive oil. Add the peeled shallots and salt and cook on a very low heat, allowing the fat to barely bubble, for 30–40 minutes, or until the shallots have completely softened. Use a slotted spoon to transfer them to a bowl, then splash on the red wine vinegar and set aside.

While the shallots are cooking, toss the sweet potato in the remaining olive oil and season. Place on a baking tray and roast for about 20 minutes, or until cooked.

Add a splash of oil to a frying pan over medium heat. Fry the bacon and, when it's pretty much cooked, add the maple syrup and sultanas and cook for another minute or two until the bacon is all candied in the syrup.

Melt the butter in a small saucepan over medium heat until it goes nutty brown – don't let it burn. Remove from the heat and squeeze in the lemon juice.

Arrange the sweet potato and shallots on a warm serving plate, lay the bacon and sultanas on top, pour over the burnt butter and finish with a generous scattering of pecans.

TIP: *Serve this sweet potato salad with roast chicken, roast corn or just a grain and green salad.*

PERFECT SAVOURY TART^

AND A BONUS SOUFFLÉ!

Hint: it's all about the pastry! Life is about building up a collection of things that you can rely on: friends, a car that always starts, your topspin backhand return, and a rough puff recipe that is just as rock-solid and reliable. Given that there is more panic about pastry than the other aforementioned items, I recommend making friends with this recipe for rough puff pastry that has stood by me through the good and bad times over the years. Just follow the simple steps below. This recipe makes about 600 g pastry.

Rough puff pastry
250g plain flour
½ teaspoon salt
200g cold butter, diced
1 tablespoon lemon juice

2. Add the butter to the flour and cut it in using two knives. The butter should remain quite lumpy.

4. Add the lemon juice to 120 ml iced water and pour it into the flour. A little acid helps keep your pastry tender.

1. Sift the flour into a large bowl and add the salt.

3. You can also use your fingers to pinch in the butter.

5. Mix it in using the knives.

9. On a well-floured surface, roll out the dough into a long rectangle, about 30 x 15 cm.

12. Repeat this process at least five times, which will build the layers of your pastry.

TIP: *You can freeze this dough and keep for up to 2 months.*

6. Give the pastry a quick knead to bring it together, but it should still be quite lumpy.

SEVEN BONUS QUICHE TIPS

☞ Cold machines are better than hot little fingers.

☞ Don't overwork the dough – this develops the gluten and makes your pastry tough.

☞ Always blind bake your pastry cases, to avoid a doughy bottom. For the same reason, never add fillings while hot.

☞ Seal any tiny holes in the pastry with beaten egg. For bigger holes, use leftover pastry trimmings.

☞ Ingredients with lots of water in them, like mushrooms, supermarket bacon, onions and tomatoes, should be cooked to dry out excess moisture before adding to your quiche filling.

☞ Fill your quiche in the oven – this will stop the filling slopping out.

☞ Don't trust the recipe timing. A quiche is cooked perfectly when the centre of the filling is no longer liquid and is just set, so watch for this moment to happen.

7. Turn the pastry out onto a floured surface and quickly shape it into a rectangle.

10. Sprinkle with a little flour, then fold one-third of the dough into the centre and fold the other third over that.

8. Wrap it in plastic wrap and place it in the fridge for an hour or so.

11. Give the dough a quarter turn and repeat, by rolling out the dough into a long rectangle, sprinkling with a little flour and re-folding.

MUSHROOM TART

Serves 6

The rough puff pastry used in this recipe is a perfect way of showing off in the kitchen without too much trouble. It's a great multi-purpose recipe to learn for sweet or savoury purposes. Here, it's used to make a sort of cross between a savoury tarte tatin and a puff pastry pizza. It's very delicious … but do make sure you use mushrooms with dark gills on the underside of the caps, as this will make the tart look so much more delicious!

2 tablespoons olive oil
6 thyme sprigs, leaves picked
8 small flat mushrooms, stalks removed,
  or 3 large portobello mushrooms
1 small red onion, thickly sliced
50 g butter
2 garlic cloves, crushed
100 g feta (soft marinated feta is best),
  roughly crumbled
Rough Puff Pastry (see page 54)

Preheat the oven to 200°C.

Heat the olive oil in a non-stick, ovenproof frying pan, about 24 cm wide.

Sprinkle some of the thyme leaves into the hot oil, then add the mushrooms, undersides facing down, along with the onion pieces and leave them to cook for about 5 minutes.

Meanwhile, melt the butter in a small saucepan and add the crushed garlic. Cook for a minute or two until fragrant, then remove from the heat.

Fill in the gaps between the mushrooms with about two-thirds of the marinated feta. Pour on the garlic butter and remove the pan from the heat.

Roll out the pastry and cut out a circle large enough to generously cover the mushrooms. Lift the pastry onto the pan and tuck it in around the edges using the tip of a wooden spoon. Bake in the oven for around 25 minutes, or until the pastry is puffed and golden brown.

Remove the tart from the oven and run a knife around the edges of the tart to make sure it's not stuck to the pan. Then place a large flat serving plate on top of the pan and flip it over. Sprinkle on the remaining feta and thyme leaves and serve hot or cold.

NOTE: *Leftover rough puff can be wrapped in plastic wrap and kept in the freezer for up to 2 months. This Mushroom Tart recipe will use roughly half of the quantity yielded by the Rough Puff Pastry recipe on page 54.*

QUICHE LORRAINE

Serves 6–8

I know it's stupid, but about twelve years ago I got it into my head that the word 'quiche' sounded like 'kiss' – if said when a bit tiddly and trying to get amorous with a barmaid called Lorraine. Obviously that is stupid, but then … so am I. And I should stop writing this stream of consciousness stuff before you realise that I am actually as shallow as a puddle on a hot day in Mildura. What I should really say is, 'Make this quiche, because it is one of those things (like cornflakes and cold milk) that you forget how good it is until you try it again!'

Oh, and this recipe is loaded with really good secrets for perfect quiche and tart making.

PASTRY
250 g plain flour
½ teaspoon salt flakes
190 g butter, diced
2 small eggs (use 1 for brushing the pastry)

FILLING
olive oil, for frying
200 g kaiserfleisch or bacon (uncooked), sliced about 4 mm thick
1 × 200 g tub crème fraîche
150 ml milk
2 eggs
2 egg yolks
150 g gruyère, grated
4 grates of fresh nutmeg
salt flakes and freshly ground black pepper

For the pastry, blitz the flour, salt and butter in your food processor until it resembles coarse breadcrumbs. Yes, I know it's contrary to the received wisdom of the granny skills movement, who espouse the use of just the right hand for pastry, but using a processor is quicker and colder than using your hands. Especially when you've got big hot hands like mine. This is an important SECRET.

Beat one of the eggs lightly, then add it to the flour and process until the mixture just comes together. Tip it onto a clean surface and, if necessary, quickly knead it into a ball. Wrap in plastic wrap and refrigerate for at least 30 minutes. This lets the gluten in the flour relax, making for more tender pastry. There's another SECRET!

Preheat the oven to 180°C and grease a 22 × 3–4 cm loose-bottomed tart tin.

For the filling, heat a little oil in a small frying pan. If using kaiserfleisch, then fry it for just a few minutes so as not to dry it out. If you have supermarket bacon you will need to fry it for a bit longer as it will contain a lot more water and you will *need* to dry it out. Once cooked, remove it from the pan and leave to cool.

Combine the crème fraîche and milk in a bowl and whisk them together to combine. Add the eggs and yolks and whisk again. You can add the cooled bacon at any time to allow the flavour to infuse the cream. Add the grated cheese, nutmeg and seasonings and pour into the tart shell.

Roll out your dough and lift it onto the prepared tin. Line the pastry with foil or baking paper and fill with baking beans or rice. Blind bake the base of the tart for 20 minutes. This will stop your tart having a doughy bottom. That's your third key SECRET in this recipe – albeit one that could perhaps be phrased a little better, so as to avoid puerile sniggering from your partner who's reading this over your shoulder.

When the tart shell comes out of the oven, remove the foil and baking beans. Lightly beat the remaining egg and use it to brush over the base to seal it. Place the tart shell back into the oven on a baking tray (SECRET!) and pour in your filling (SECRET!). Bake for 30–40 minutes, or until the centre of the tart is no longer liquid (SLIGHTLY OBVIOUS SECRET). The cooking time can vary so keep an eye on it.

The quiche can be served immediately or reheated at a later time.

FINAL SECRET: *Kaiserfleisch can be bought from a good German or Austrian butcher and has a strong smoky-bacon flavour that works perfectly in this tart. You will also find it in larger supermarkets and decent butchers these days. It is also one of the most widely used ingredients in this book.*

JALAPEÑO AND CHEDDAR SOUFFLÉS

Serves 4

No other recipe in this book has caused more angst than this one. However, the magic flavour of plump green jalapeños made it worth perfecting. You can make this as one large soufflé, but individual is just so much better!

40 g butter, softened, plus extra
25 g parmesan, finely grated
8 fresh jalapeño chillies (long green chillies can be substituted), deseeded

70 g pickled jalapeño chillies
40 ml jalapeño brine (from the jar)
2 heaped teaspoons plain flour
140 g cheddar (the bitiest you can find),

120 g grated, 20 g cut into small dice
2 egg yolks
7 egg whites
1 teaspoon caster sugar

Use a pastry brush to paint some of the butter up the sides of 4 small china ramekins. Place the ramekins in the fridge to chill. When chilled, brush on more butter in upwards strokes to create a sort of tramline effect. These 'butter rails' will help the soufflé to rise neatly (SECRET).

Sprinkle a quarter of the grated parmesan into the first ramekin. Hold it on an angle and rotate it, so the parmesan sticks to the butter in a fine layer. Tip any excess parmesan into the next ramekin and repeat until all the ramekins have coated sides. Return to the fridge.

Preheat the oven to 200°C.

Dice 3 of the fresh chillies and set aside for garnish. Roughly chop the other 5 and blitz them with the pickled jalapeños and the pickling brine, which will give you about 125 ml of pickle mixture to flavour your soufflés.

Make a roux by melting 40 g butter in a small saucepan and then stirring in the flour until it forms a paste. Slowly add dollops of the pickle mix, stirring it in well. When it has all been incorporated, stir in the grated cheddar until it melts and the mixture looks like a thick paste. Remove the pan from the heat and stir in the egg yolks until combined. Keep this chilli-cheese base mixture warm as it's easier to incorporate into the egg whites that way (SECRET).

Whisk the egg whites with the sugar on medium speed until they form soft peaks. Don't over-whip or you will get a soufflé that rises but then quickly collapses (SECRET).

Warm and dry a large mixing bowl. Add the warm jalapeño and cheese base and cut – or fold – in 1 tablespoon of the whisked egg whites to prepare the base. A large thin, flat metal spoon is best for this. The main aim is to not knock out any of the air from the whites. Also preparing the base with a little of the egg whites first will help with smooth incorporation (SECRET). Add half of the remaining egg whites and fold them in until incorporated. Repeat with the rest of the whites.

Bring a full kettle to the boil and line a deep baking tray with a folded tea towel. The tea towel keeps the ramekins flat, insulates the bottoms and stops any wobbling that might impede the rise (3 SECRETS!). The tray should be large enough to hold 4 ramekins without touching.

Remove the ramekins from the fridge and fill them with the soufflé mixture. Tap them on the bench to help the mixture settle, then smooth the surface of the mixture in each ramekin (SECRET, SECRET). Run your thumbnail around the soufflé mix at the rim of the ramekins – or use the blunt edge of a knife. This flattened edge and separation of top from rim will encourage a clean rise and minimise the issue of tilted or toppled soufflés (SECRET).

Call your guests to the table. This soufflé will settle after 3 minutes, so you want people ready and waiting!

Arrange the filled ramekins in the baking tray and place it in the oven. Carefully pour in boiled water from the kettle so it comes halfway up the sides of the ramekins, then bake for 10 minutes. The water will ensure a gentler, more even cook.

Check through the glass to see if they are starting to rise (whew!) and call your guests to the table again – but with bordering-on-hysterical urgency. Leave the soufflés in the oven for 2 more minutes. This will give you a gooey soufflé. If you want a firmer, golden edged soufflé give them 5 more minutes, or for ones that you can turn out onto a board to eat with a salad, then keep them in for another 7 minutes (i.e. a total baking time of 17 or 19 minutes, respectively).

Remove the soufflés from the oven, sprinkle the surface of each with the diced fresh chilli and diced cheddar and eat straight away with crusty bread 'n' butter and a green salad.

PEA AND GOAT'S CHEESE FRITTATA

Serves 8–10

I love frozen peas, and this Sicilian twist on a classic frittata – black pepper, peas and eggs are such a brilliant combo – shows off their beauty to great impact. The mint comes from the Englishman in me; the dill and the mint from the Greek!

300 g frozen baby peas
3 tablespoons olive oil
8 eggs
1 × 200 g tub crème fraîche
salt flakes and freshly ground
 black pepper
4 heaped tablespoons finely sliced
 spring onions
4 heaped tablespoons chopped dill
4 heaped tablespoons chopped mint
100 g best-quality creamy goat's cheese

Preheat the oven to 190°C.

Bring a saucepan of water to the boil and blanch the peas for about 10 seconds. Drain them well and set aside.

Heat the olive oil in a non-stick, ovenproof frying pan, about 24 cm wide.

Whisk the eggs with the crème fraîche and season with salt and pepper. Add the spring onion and fresh herbs.

Pour the egg mixture into the frying pan and scatter in the peas. Dot large chunks of the goat cheese around the pan. Place in the oven and bake for 15–20 minutes, or until the centre is just cooked through.

To serve, run a knife around the edge of the frittata, place a large flat serving plate on top of the pan and flip it over. The frittata should come out cleanly. Invert it again onto a serving plate, give it a final season with salt and pepper and serve.

PERFECT PIE

What recipes scare me the most? That's simple – the ones with only a couple of ingredients that are totally transformed in the cooking process. At the summit of these terrors sits pastry, which, at its most basic, is no more than two parts flour and one part fat. But there are many tricky spots where a misstep will see your pastry end up soggy, tooth-snappingly tough or just falling apart. That's why you need knowledge and technique to succeed. So here is everything that you need to know to make good pastry – the secret to the perfect pie.

WHY THE FAT MATTERS

SECRET #3: In shortcrust pastry, fat is added not just for flavour, but also to stop gluten development. The fat basically coats the flour and stops these proteins forming bonds to create gluten. That's why we always rub butter into the flour before adding any liquids. With flaky or puff pastry, you'll note, the butter isn't rubbed in, but left in chunks. When very cold butter melts in the oven it leaves air pockets between the pastry layers after they have firmed, resulting in loads of crisp, flaky layers. The evaporation of water in the butter also creates steam, which helps the puffing up.

WHY THE FLOUR MATTERS

SECRET #1: The choice of ingredients is vital for the type of pastry you want to make. For a basic sweet or savoury pastry, when you want a tender crust and a crumbly finish, you need to inhibit the development of gluten. Gluten is created when, helped by water, two flour proteins (glutelin and gliadin) bond through pressure, manipulation and stretching of the dough. Softer flour with less protein will increase your chances of making a shortcrust pastry that is crumbly rather than tough. Ordinary plain flour is fine. Adding a little strong, higher protein bread flour to your plain flour can be a good idea when making puff pastry, as it helps the sheets of gluten develop that will end up as your flaky layers separated by butter, which helps them lift and separate into a many-layered jamboree of flakiness.

WHY TEMPERATURE MATTERS

SECRET #2: Water mixed with flour helps swell the flour granules so they can then form gluten, but gluten is the enemy of tender pastry. Water is absorbed into flour proteins less easily, however, when the temperature is colder, and this is why pastry purists recommend cold ingredients, cold equipment and marble boards. Keeping the butter cold also helps when making shortcrust pastry because it doesn't melt into the flour when you are working it in. With puff, cold butter provides the vital barrier and air pockets between the pastry layers that transforms into delicious flakiness. Cold hands and a cold kitchen also help, which is why Grandma's pastry was often better: she didn't have heating in the kitchen. Colder still are the blades of a food processor!

WHY THE SUGAR MATTERS

SECRET #4: Sure, I get that sugar adds sweetness to a sweet shortcrust pastry, but I could never understand why my sweet pastry was often better than my savoury shortcrust. Then Russ Parsons, one of my favourite food writers, explained it: adding sugar helps protect the flour from the water that you then add to bring it together, thereby again reducing gluten formation.

BE CAREFUL WORKING THE DOUGH

SECRET #7: Shortcrust pastry is like your girlfriend – it needs to be treated gently and with respect if you want it to be tender. Pressure also helps gluten develop, which is why recipes always ask you to just pull the dough together gently and to work it minimally for a short or crumbly result. When rolling out pastry, remember to roll away from you, don't put downward pressure on the dough, and don't over-roll.

With puff pastry, however, it is all about the rolling because you want to develop sheets of gluten. More accurately, it is about the rolling and folding, because you want thin layers of strong pastry separated by butter. Every time you roll and fold your puff pastry, you multiply the layers of butter and pastry by three. So after five turns, you'll have a spectacular two hundred and forty-four layers. Rotate, roll and fold again and you'll have more than seven hundred layers. Epic.

REST THE PASTRY

SECRET #8: Resting the pastry in the fridge for at least 15 minutes – but ideally 30 minutes or more – before blind baking allows the gluten to relax and the pastry to chill. Cool, relaxed pastry and gluten means your pastry is far more likely to hold its shape when cooking.

If your chilled pastry seems too stiff to roll out, give it a couple of whacks with the rolling pin to shock it into rollable submission, but don't try and make it warm up. And drape the pastry over your rolling pin to move it onto the tray or flan case; it's much gentler this way.

WHY ACID MATTERS

SECRET #5: Adding acid to your pastry, in the form of sour cream or a little lemon juice, helps retard the development of the gluten and makes for a more tender result.

WHY BLIND BAKE

SECRET #9: Soggy bottoms are a common problem for tarts, especially those with looser custard fillings such as a quiche or a lemon tart. Baking the tart crust before filling it – blind baking it – allows it to repel moisture and stay firm. After lining the tin with pastry, cover it with a sheet of foil or baking paper and fill with rice, baking weights, or even a new metal dog chain. Bake in a preheated 180°C oven for 10 minutes, then remove the weights and the paper/foil and return it to the oven to go a little golden.

ADD YOUR WATER GRADUALLY

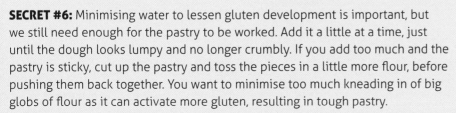

SECRET #6: Minimising water to lessen gluten development is important, but we still need enough for the pastry to be worked. Add it a little at a time, just until the dough looks lumpy and no longer crumbly. If you add too much and the pastry is sticky, cut up the pastry and toss the pieces in a little more flour, before pushing them back together. You want to minimise too much kneading in of big globs of flour as it can activate more gluten, resulting in tough pastry.

BEEF AND ONION PIE

Makes 6

Now, you can always top this pie with my normal shortcrust or sour cream pastry but as it's usually for a bit of a special occasion – and therefore a rarity – when you roll this spectacular pie out, do try the lard version below. It makes for a very fine pastry indeed. Just don't make a habit of it!!!

For the best results, do also make the beef filling the day before. It doesn't take long in total, but you'll need to allocate little periods of time for various jobs over a day or so!! While we are getting all over excited and using multiple exclamation marks, can I also point out that the secret to this recipe – other than the lard – is the use of dates (!!) and malt vinegar (!!!), which add a wonderful richness and complexity to the beef gravy!!!!

3 tablespoons olive oil
3 onions, sliced
2 garlic cloves, crushed
1 kg chuck steak (not too lean), cubed
500 ml (2 cups) beef stock
80 g pitted dates, puréed with a little water
2 ½ tablespoons malt vinegar
2 bay leaves
salt flakes and freshly ground black pepper

PASTRY
600 g plain flour
1 teaspoon salt flakes
170 g very cold butter
170 g very cold lard
1 egg, beaten (for brushing)

Preheat the oven to 200ºC.

Heat the oil in a large flameproof casserole. Fry the onion over medium heat until soft, translucent and beginning to caramelise. Add the garlic and fry for a minute, then tip everything out of the casserole and set aside.

In the same casserole, fry the meat in batches to brown it.

Return the onion and all the meat to the casserole. Pour in the stock and add the remaining ingredients. Cover with a tight-fitting lid and cook in the oven for 2 ½ hours. Remove from the oven and shred the meat with a fork. Place in the fridge for a few hours (or overnight) to cool completely.

At least 2 hours before you want to eat, make the pastry. Combine the flour and salt in a food processor and add the butter and lard. Pulse briefly until the butter is still a little lumpy, with some pieces around the size of small peas. Tip into a large bowl, add 170 ml ice-cold water and mix until the pastry just comes together as a dough. Turn out onto a clean work surface and knead the pastry briefly before wrapping in plastic wrap. Place in the fridge to rest for an hour or so.

Preheat the oven to 200ºC.

Roll out two-thirds of the pastry and line six individual pie tins, leaving an overhang to trim later. Spoon in the beef filling.

Roll out the remaining dough and cut out six lids. Brush the exposed pastry rims with the egg wash and place the lids on top. Trim the edges neatly and pinch the pastry around the edges of the pies to seal. Bake in the oven for 30 minutes, then serve warm.

MRS WOOLTON'S PIE

Serves 10–12

This pie was invented in war-torn Britain to make the most of the ration-book diet. It's a pretty dour dish in its original form, but this version steps things up a bit by using butter and cheese to thicken the sauce and by replacing the original potato pastry with a more decadent short crust. At its heart, this winter dish is still all about a mass of deliciously juicy, soft veggies under golden pastry; it's just a bit softer and toastier than the more austere original, which was named after the wartime minister for rationing and originally made at the Savoy. That's the reason I named this recipe for his wife – who I am sure would have improved Lord Woolton's original idea this way.

And yes, it's good for vegetarians too! Depending on the cheese and the pastry you choose, obviously.

80 g butter
2 onions, chopped
2 leeks, white parts only, washed and finely sliced
300 g potatoes, cut into 3 cm chunks
300 g parsnips, cut into 3 cm chunks
200 g swede, cut into 3 cm chunks
400 g carrots, cut into 3 cm chunks
300 g cauliflower florets
500 ml (2 cups) chicken stock
1 bunch of of flat-leaf parsley, leaves picked and chopped
2 tablespoons oatmeal
1 heaped tablespoon plain flour
1 tablespoon Keen's or Colman's mustard powder
100 g gruyère or flavourful cheddar (optional)

PASTRY
300 g plain flour
1 teaspoon salt flakes
80 g very cold butter, diced
80 g very cold lard, diced

For the pastry, combine the flour, salt, butter and lard in the bowl of your food processor and blitz, leaving it a little bit lumpy. Tip into a mixing bowl, add 3 ½ tablespoons of iced water and bring it together into a dough. Tip onto a floured surface and shape into a disc. Wrap in plastic wrap and refrigerate for an hour or so.

Heat half the butter in a large, heavy-bottomed saucepan and fry the onion until soft. Add the leek and cook, covered, for a few minutes. Throw in all the remaining veg – except the cauliflower – and stir into the onion. Fry for 5 minutes until they get the occasional, lightly tanned edge. Pour in the stock and simmer, covered, for 30 minutes. Add the cauliflower at the 20-minute mark.

Drain the veg, taking care to reserve all the stock, then layer them in a large pie dish, sprinkling in the parsley and oatmeal as you go.

Preheat the oven to 180°C.

Melt the rest of the butter in the same saucepan. Stir in the flour and mustard powder and let it toast a little, but keep stirring. Add a cup of the reserved stock and mix it in well, still over the heat. As it thickens, add the rest of the stock in batches, until it is a good spoon-coating consistency. If you are using cheese, you can stir it in now. Check the seasoning and adjust with more salt if necessary. Pour the sauce onto the veg.

Roll the pastry out to the shape of your pie dish, with enough to overhang the edges. Lift it on top and crimp the edges. Don't forget to make a couple of holes in the top for the steam to escape. Bang it in the oven. It's done when the pastry is cooked and golden; about 30 minutes, say I.

Serve with green beans, in an air-raid shelter with the distant drone of Daimler Benz engines from a squadron of Dorniers filling the air – and even then all will seem right with the world.

THE 11 SIMPLE SECRETS TO THE

PERFECT SEAFOOD

I asked Rick Stein to pick his three best seafood tips. Here they are! Thanks, Rick – you are my seafood Obi-Wan Kenobi. I once called you my seafood Yoda and then I realised afterwards that this might not have come across quite as I intended. For the record, you are neither short, green nor wrinkled – you just know loads about seafood and other stuff.

SLOWLY DOES IT

RICK SECRET #2: Cook fish on a slower heat for longer, rather than hard and fast. You need to treat fish gently; it's delicate!

EIGHT OTHER KEY SECRETS I'VE LEARNT ABOUT FISH

USE A THERMOMETER

RICK SECRET #1: Use a thermometer to check when your fish is cooked (55°C is underdone and 70°C is overdone). And remember that fish continues to cook after it's taken off the heat or out of the pan, so always err towards underdone.

BUY FRESH

MATT SECRET #1: The freshest fish has clear, bright, raised eyes, it smells of the sea and the flesh springs back when squeezed. The gills should be red. Don't buy a fish if the gills have been cut out or are brown, or if it smells like a Paris pissoir on a hot August's day.

USE FENNEL

RICK SECRET #3: Roast or steam whole fish over wild fennel or fennel. (Rick has a bit of a thing about fennel . . . and tarragon, actually . . . and Pernod . . . and star anise . . .).

DON'T BUY

MATT SECRET #2: . . . the marinated fish you find at the fishmonger or supermarket. It's never, ever as tasty as it sounds.

EAT IT TODAY

MATT SECRET #5: It ain't going to get any fresher!

STEAM OR BRAISE FILLETS

MATT SECRET #7: Never poach a fish fillet. It's far better to steam it or to braise it in a rich stew or sauce.

WILD IS BEST

MATT SECRET #3: Wild fish usually tastes better and has a better texture than farmed fish – just pick a wild fish that isn't endangered.

LOVE YOUR FISHMONGER

MATT SECRET #4: Do find a good fish shop and make friends with the fishmonger. Trust in his expertise. Ask him, 'What's great today?' and if he says, 'The flathead,' then buy it. If he says, 'The teriyaki salmon skewers,' then find a new fishmonger.

SAVE MONEY

MATT SECRET #6: Save money and poach whole fish in salted water rather than in stock, which will only add minimal flavour. One teaspoon of salt for every 600 ml of water is the ideal ratio.

ROAST WHOLE FISH

MATT SECRET #8: Roast fish at 200°C and cook it for 10 minutes for every 2.5 cm of thickness. This comes from the old Canadian rule of thumb, which says 10 minutes for every inch (measured at the thickest part of the fish or fillet). Turn it over halfway through this calculated cooking time. Thin fillets (less than 1.25 cm) don't need to be turned. Fish cooked in foil or baking paper will need an extra 5 minutes.

JUST A SIMPLE SEAFOOD STEW

Serves 4

Oh, how we grow up. Back when I was four, the very mention of a fish stew would have me barricading myself in the cubbyhouse with enough mud pies to last a sizeable siege – at least until bedtime. These days I think a fish stew is actually rather nice, but the key is finding a fishmonger you can trust, going gently with both the heat and the flavourings and using seafood so fresh it passes comment on how hot you bum looks in those pants and then winks at you suggestively.

3 large potatoes, peeled and cut into thick slices
1 litre (4 cups) fish stock
3 ½ tablespoons olive oil
1 onion, finely diced
1 fennel bulb, sliced finely lengthways, nicest fronds reserved
4 garlic cloves, finely chopped
1 celery stalk, finely sliced
2 fresh bay leaves
250 ml (1 cup) white wine
2 calamari, cleaned, tubes cut into rings, tentacles cut into pairs, long ones halved
1 blue swimmer crab, cleaned and quartered
4 jumbo raw prawns, heads and shells on
500 g tomatoes, blanched, peeled and chopped
350 ml passata
500 g firm-fleshed fish fillet (blue eye, sea perch or red mullet), cut into large chunks
16 smallish black mussels, cleaned
1 rustic baguette, toasted (see NOTE)

Cook the discs of potato in 500 ml of fish stock until they are just falling apart. Drain and set aside.

Heat the olive oil in a large heavy-based flameproof casserole over low–medium heat. Add the onion, fennel, garlic, celery and bay leaves and sauté for about 10 minutes, or until soft. Add the wine and bring to a simmer for 5 minutes.

Add the calamari rings and tentacles to the casserole and cook for 2 minutes. Remove them from the pan and reserve.

Add the crab, prawns and tomatoes to the casserole and toss over the heat for 2–3 minutes.

Remove the crab and prawns from the casserole and set aside with the calamari.

Pour the remaining 500 ml of fish stock into the casserole, along with the passata, and bring to a gentle boil. Carefully add the white fish chunks to the fishy, tomatoey deliciousness and poach for 5 minutes.

Add all the cooked seafood (and any juices) and the potatoes back to the casserole and cook for a few minutes.

Finally, add the mussels, cover with a lid and cook until the shells open – it will take around 3 minutes, by which time all the seafood and potatoes should be hot and cooked through. Top with the reserved fennel fronds and serve at the table for people to share. Otherwise, serve it up in big bowls. Either way, don't forget the bread to mop up all the soup.

NOTE: As an option, you can slice the baguette thinly on an angle and chargrill the slices. Rub them with a clove of garlic after they are all toasty brown.

THE WORLD IN BLACK AND WHITE – A DISH STOLEN, IN PART, FROM A FISH-OBSESSED ENGLISHMAN AND A CRAZY BASQUE FROM PARIS

Serves 6–8

The Melbourne Food and Wine Festival has always had a bit of a love affair with squid ink. Inaki Aizpitarte used it to make arroz negra and more recently, Mitch Tonks, from one of the UK's top three seafood restaurants, turned his hand to cuttlefish with crunchy polenta chips. My recipe takes inspiration from both of these great cooks, but uses calamari – which is ironic given how plentiful cuttlefish are at my local beach. Sadly, they seemed to be non-existent in the fish shops when I was testing this recipe!

olive oil
3 small onions, finely sliced
2 celery stalks, finely chopped
2 fennel bulbs, finely chopped, nicest fronds reserved
4 garlic cloves, finely chopped
3 bay leaves
2 green chillies, deseeded and pith removed, diced
½ bunch of oregano, leaves chopped

1 teaspoon fennel seeds (or ½ teaspoon fennel pollen), crushed
750 ml (1 bottle) shiraz
300 g cherry tomatoes
½ bunch of flat-leaf parsley, leaves and stalks very finely chopped
1 kg fresh calamari tubes, cleaned and skinned (or frozen tubes, thawed), sliced crossways into 5 mm rings
2 tablespoons squid ink (or cuttlefish ink)

salt flakes, if needed
2 tablespoons red wine vinegar

WHITE POLENTA
225 g (1 ½ cups) polenta
750 ml (1 bottle) Aussie riesling
750 ml (3 cups) fish stock or water
1 × 200 g tub crème fraîche
½ bunch of flat-leaf parsley, leaves picked and finely chopped

Set a large saucepan on medium heat and pour in enough olive oil to coat the bottom. Fry the onion, celery and fennel until they start to soften. Throw in the garlic, 2 bay leaves and the green chilli and cook for 5 minutes until soft. Stir in the oregano and the fennel seeds. Rack up the heat. Pour in a cup of red wine and cook until you have deglazed the pan and the wine has completely evaporated. Pour in the rest of the wine, bring to the boil, then scrape into a bowl and reserve.

Add more oil to the same pan and fry the tomatoes for about 5 minutes, until they break down. Throw in the parsley. Stir and cook for a minute or two until wilted. Tip into the bowl with the onion mixture.

Add a little more oil to the pan, add the calamari and fry it for 3 minutes. I say 'fry' but, really, unless you are going to do this in batches it will stew not fry. But that's OK. Just pour any calamari juices into the onion mix as they are rendered.

Blitz the onion and wine mixture into a gravy with a stick blender or a blender (which will give you a smoother result). Pour it over the calamari; it may sizzle and spit initially. Stir in the squid ink and the last bay leaf. Turn the

heat down to a bare simmer and cook for about an hour, uncovered, or until the calamari is super-tender and the sauce is black and glossy.

Taste and season only now, as the saltiness of squid ink can intensify as the sauce cooks down. Also add the red wine vinegar.

When you're ready to cook the polenta, heat a little olive oil in a large saucepan. Add the polenta and stir over medium heat for about 5 minutes, until it looks like wet sand and has a toasted maizy smell. Don't let it catch or burn!

Check your polenta packet for the correct liquid ratio, then make that liquid half wine and half stock (or water). Pour the required amount of wine into a large saucepan and bring to the boil. Then simmer, uncovered, for 5 minutes. Add the fish stock (or water) and bring to the boil again. Now add the polenta in a steady stream, whisking all the time, then cook as per the packet instructions. At the last minute, stir most of the crème fraîche into the polenta.

Serve the black calamari on the white polenta, garnished with the parsley and the reserved fennel fronds. Finish with a dollop of the remaining crème fraîche.

MUSSELS AND CANNELLINI BEANS

Serves 2

If the Inuit peoples have a hundred words for snow, I'm the same with texture. I love the subtle differences between wet crunch, toasty crunch, friable crunch, nutty crunch and just plain crunchy crunch – but more than that, what I love is all the different ways that creaminess manifests itself other than just in a dollop of cream. This dish is all about that creaminess – and it doesn't use any cream: it's the creaminess of the inside of those white beans; the creaminess of the just-cooked mussel flesh; the creaminess that comes from marrying the tender flesh of ripe tomatoes with some of the rendered fat from a chorizo sausage. So luxuriate in this simple peasant dish, inspired by long lunches spent in cheap bars around Spain. Serve it with a cider that has a suitably soft and creamy mousse (that's a few small bubbles – or lightly carbonated – to you and me!) and a soft-crumb bread with loads of creamy butter.

1 fresh chorizo sausage, finely diced
extra-virgin olive oil
1 small onion, diced
3 garlic cloves, diced
200 ml wine
1 × 400 g can cannellini beans,
  rinsed and drained
400 g tomatoes, diced
1 kg mussels, scrubbed clean and
  beards removed
¼ bunch of flat-leaf parsley, leaves
  picked and finely chopped
10 green olives, pitted and diced
grilled slices of crusty bread, to serve

Sauté the chorizo in a large, deep frying pan over high heat until coloured and crunchy. Set aside.

Wipe out any excess chorizo fat in the pan and add 2 tablespoons of extra-virgin olive oil. Fry the onion and garlic over medium heat until they soften, but don't let them colour too much. Add the wine and 200 ml of water and bring to the boil, then reduce the heat to a simmer.

In a second large pan, add another splash of olive oil over medium heat and add the beans and tomato. When hot, add half the cooked chorizo.

Go back to the simmering pan of onion–garlic liquid and add the mussels. Cover the pan and reduce the heat to a simmer. Cook for just a couple of minutes until the mussels open, tossing the pan at least once.

Pour the mussels and most, if not all, of the liquid onto the tomatoey beans and simmer for another minute. Look, it all depends on how runny you want your sauce. There's no wrong or right way here. For example, if you are the sort of person who likes to mash their beans into the sauce, then a looser sauce is desirable. But if you are a flavour junkie, then you don't want to dilute that rich tomatoey goodness too much!

Mix the parsley with the olives. When you're ready to serve, scatter the rest of the chorizo onto the mussels, followed by the parsley and olives. Finish with a drizzle of oil and serve with crusty bread to mop up all the juices.

PERFECT PRAWNS

At their best, prawns are amongst the finest things to eat on this earth. At their worst, they are amongst the very worst! Here are my secrets to how to make eating prawns a joy every time.

DEFROST THEM PROPERLY

SECRET #1: Take frozen prawns out of their packaging, put on a plate and thaw them slowly in the fridge over 24 hours. If you have forgotten to thaw your prawns, don't thaw them in water or use the microwave . . . just relax, make something else instead and eat the prawns later!

PICK A GOOD PRAWN

SECRET #3: Choose prawns that smell sweet and mildly of the sea, that look vibrant and fresh and feel firm. Reject any that have a hint of fishiness or ammonia, or that are dry, slimy or speckled with black. These black splotches may not be due to age or the prawns being treated with metabisulphite but it's just not worth taking a risk. You, as the consumer, after all, have the right to choose! (Basically what I am saying is that black prawns may be OK to eat and not be old or treated with metabisulphite, but why take the risk?)

HOW MANY PRAWNS DO I NEED?

SECRET #5: Remember that 1 kg of prawns in the shell will yield 500 g of prawn meat.

WASTE NOTHING

SECRET #6: Never throw out the heads, legs or shells. The heads and legs of green prawns can be barbecued or fried for a crispy snack or garnish. You can also fry the shells, heads and legs in a little oil and then strain off and save the tasty prawn-flavoured oil. Or else deglaze the pan with white wine, reduce, then pour in enough water to cover all the bits and simmer. Strain to make a prawn stock and freeze it until you need it.

DON'T REFREEZE

SECRET #2: Please don't refreeze once-frozen prawns, or anything that you make using them. Remember that many of the prawns sold in supermarkets have already been frozen.

ALWAYS BUY GREEN PRAWNS

SECRET #4: If you want to cook prawns, then buy green (raw) prawns, either fresh or frozen. Those pink, ready-cooked prawns are only good for using in blander salads or for mounding up to dunk into aioli.

THE EASY WAY TO PEEL A PRAWN

SECRET #7: To shell a prawn, first twist off the head,

then use scissors to snip off the shell by cutting along one side of the belly

Slip out the flesh.

DON'T OVERCOOK 'EM

SECRET #9: Prawns require very little cooking to become springy, sweet and succulent. They will stir-fry in a couple of minutes, barbecue in about 4 minutes and poach in 3–8 minutes, depending on size.

ALWAYS REMOVE THE POO SHOOT

SECRET #8: Remove the poo shoot either by cutting along the back of the prawn to lift it out (which is quickest)

or by making a small incision on the back near the tail and using a skewer to hook it out. You'll need to ease it out very gently. This is fiddly and slower but far neater.

WHEN NOT TO SHELL

SECRET #10: Barbecue or grill prawns in the shell and then peel them after cooking to protect the meat and ensure that they are juicier and bolder in flavour.

ONE FINAL SECRET TO MAKE YOUR NEIGHBOURS LOVE YOU MORE

SECRET #11: If it's not bin night, wrap up any leftover prawn detritus tightly in a plastic bag and place in the freezer until it is bin night. A bin full of prawn heads that have rotted over five successive 30°C days is truly horrific to anyone within 50 metres.

WE LOVE YOU TOADY

PRAWN COCKTAIL

Serves 4

Call me a dag, but I love the flavours in a prawn cocktail. Over the last couple of books I've played with making this brilliant combo 'cool', but have never actually celebrated the classic archetype on which these riffs were based. I redress that oversight right here, right now! Oh, but I've added wedges of avocado because I love its creaminess against the creaminess of the cocktail sauce and the prawn flesh. (You see I wasn't lying about my love of creaminess back on page 77!)

2 French shallots, diced as finely
  as possible
salt flakes
2 teaspoons brandy
1 lemon, peeled and segmented
1 teaspoon olive oil
4–6 iceberg lettuce leaves, finely
  shredded
20 king prawns, cooked and peeled, with
  tails intact
2 avocados, peeled, halved and each
  half sliced crossways
tarragon or chervil leaves, to serve
  (optional)

COCKTAIL SAUCE
200 ml cream
juice of ½–1 lemon
2 tablespoons tomato sauce
1 tablespoon worcestershire sauce
1 teaspoon tabasco sauce
½ teaspoon salt flakes
freshly ground white pepper,
  to taste

For the cocktail sauce, first, lightly whip the cream to thicken it just a little. Stir in the lemon juice, tomato sauce, worcestershire sauce and tabasco and season with salt and white pepper. Taste and adjust the seasoning, also adding more lemon juice if you think it needs it. Place in the fridge to allow the flavours to infuse into the cream.

Prepare your diced shallots. Do you think they are small enough? Of course they aren't. Cut them even smaller. Now toss the dice with a pinch of salt and the brandy and let stand for 15 minutes.

Cut the lemon segments in thirds, toss them in the oil and leave for 15 minutes. This will take the sharpness away from the citrus, but leave their gorgeous fragrance and flavour.

Time to assemble your cocktails. Take four wide-rimmed cocktail glasses and nestle some lettuce in the bottom of each. Arrange the prawn tails so they hang over the edge of the glass, placing a piece of avocado in between some of the prawns.

Spoon a generous dollop of sauce into each glass and scatter on the herbs, the citrus jewels and a few brandied shallots. Serve immediately.

PRAWN SAGANAKI

Serves 4

This is the dullest intro in the book, but it is full of facts – albeit rather magnificently dull facts! Saganaki is not fried cheese. It is actually the two-handled frying pan that my Greek chums use to fry their cheese in. They also use the saganaki pan to make this dish of prawns in tomato sauce; hence the name, 'prawn saganaki'. I use cheese in my version of this dish because I like to break rules, and there are lots of rules about not using cheese with seafood. However, I don't use the cheese they use for saganaki – which is usually graviera or kefalograviera. That would just be too confusing – and dull.

1 onion, diced
splash of olive oil
3 garlic cloves, crushed
1 lemon
1 × 400 g can tomatoes
500 g raw prawn tails, peeled and
** deveined**
100 g feta, crumbled
1 bunch of flat-leaf parsley, leaves and
** finer stalks chopped**

Preheat the oven to 180°C.

First, make a garlicky tomato sauce by cooking down the diced onion in olive oil until it is soft. Add the garlic, toss and cook for 3 minutes.

Peel off a finger-length strip of lemon zest and add along with the can of tomatoes. Cook until thick, which will take about 10 minutes.

Pop the casserole or metal pan you'll finish the saganaki in in the oven to warm. Clearly it needs to be ovenproof.

Stir the prawn tails into the sauce and when the sauce is hot again dollop it into the preheated casserole. Sprinkle the crumbled feta over the top and bake for at least 20 minutes, or until the prawns are curled up and cooked and the feta is a little brown in places. If the former happens before the latter, then give the feta a little burst under the grill.

Sprinkle with the parsley and serve with the rest of the lemon cut into small wedges and a small-grain pasta like orzo or risoni, or just with crusty bread and a chunky cucumber salad.

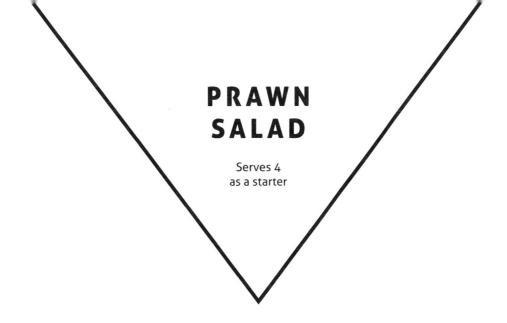

PRAWN
SALAD

Serves 4
as a starter

Every two years I indulge in my own personal little slice of happiness. It's a house on a deserted bay, down an almost impassable, almost washed-away track, on the sort of no-nonsense Queensland tropical island that's so beautiful you don't boast about it when you find it. In fact, it's so keen on remaining hidden that it throws compasses off direction when they pass. Besides the fishing, the serenity and a rather good pizza joint, there's also a great prawn fisherman on the island, so I tend to cook an awful lot of his prawns when I'm up there. This is the sort of recipe that I love to cook when I'm looking out over those azure waters from the kitchen. Everything about it sings Aussie beach holiday – even if you are cooking it in the inner-city in August. In fact, perhaps that might be the *best* time to cook this recipe, just to thrust a little sunshine back into your life, and banish the SADs.

2 tablespoons peanut oil
16 raw prawns, peeled, deveined and butterflied, with tails intact
1 teaspoon salt flakes
¼ teaspoon sesame oil
2 green mangoes, peeled and very finely sliced into threads
½ bunch of Vietnamese mint, leaves picked
½ bunch of Thai basil, leaves picked
1 lime, cut into wedges, to serve

THAI SYRUP
100 g palm sugar, chopped or grated
10 black peppercorns
2 kaffir lime leaves, torn
2 slices of ginger
1 red bullet chilli, split and deseeded
3 cm piece of lemongrass, bruised
4 very thin slices of fresh pineapple
squeeze of lime

Start with the Thai syrup. Place the palm sugar in a small saucepan with 370 ml of water. Cook over low–medium heat until the sugar dissolves, then add the peppercorns, kaffir lime, ginger, chilli, lemongrass and pineapple and bring to the boil. Simmer for about 10 minutes, then remove the pineapple and place it on a baking tray lined with baking paper.

Continue simmering the syrup until the volume has reduced by one-third and has begun to thicken a little. Remove from the heat and allow to cool. Once it is at room temperature, add a squeeze of lime.

Preheat your grill to low. Place the pineapple underneath and grill until the edges have turned all dark, sticky and caramelised. (Or pan-fry them with a little of the syrup.) Remove from the heat and leave the pineapple slices to cool.

Heat the peanut oil in a frying pan over medium–high heat. Sear the prawns on all sides, which should take 3–4 minutes. While they're cooking, sprinkle on the salt and add a few drops of sesame oil.

As soon as the prawns are cooked, assemble the salad. Toss the mango threads with a couple of tablespoons of the syrupy dressing. Add the prawns and give them a quick toss with the mango. Spoon onto a platter for serving, or divide between individual plates. Scatter on the Vietnamese mint and Thai basil. Cut the caramelised pineapple into small wedges (removing the woody core if necessary) and tuck them into the salad. Serve immediately with any leftover syrup dressing and the lime wedges on the side.

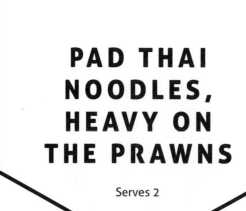

PAD THAI NOODLES, HEAVY ON THE PRAWNS

Serves 2

Done well, this is one of the world's ten best takeaway dishes – especially if you ask for extra prawns – but done badly, it can be a sludgy disaster. But now you no longer need risk the disappointment of a sub-standard pad Thai from a no-care wok, because you'll be making it yourself with this recipe!

As this is going to become a staple at your place, make the effort to go to a Thai grocer (if you've got one near where you live) to stock up on the best fish sauce, palm sugar, noodles, tamarind paste and dried shrimp. If you live in the bush, then badger the next city slickers who come to stay to bring these with them! Oh, and add in some white miso paste, gochujang, ten packets of Korean lava and a good oyster sauce. Sorry. I have nightmares – like wake-in-a-cold-sweat-type nightmares – about living deep in the outback with no access to juniper berries and chipotle. So I do get a little twitchy talking about this subject. Yes, I know this is a chilling indictment on my character; I should be having nightmares about global warming, fracking and the military industrial complex.

Anyway, the secret to good pad Thai is having all your ingredients prepped and ready to go before you start.

120 g flat rice stick noodles
4 tablespoons fish sauce
4 tablespoons tamarind pulp concentrate
80 g palm sugar, grated
pinch of chilli powder (optional)
4 tablespoons vegetable oil
2 garlic cloves, very finely chopped
10 raw prawns, shelled and deveined, with tails intact
120 g firm tofu, cut into 1.5 cm cubes
2 eggs, lightly beaten
1 ½ tablespoons dried shrimp
3–4 spring onions, chopped into small coins
50 g (⅓ cup) unsalted roasted peanuts
100 g bean shoots
coriander sprigs, to serve
lime wedges, to serve

Soak the noodles in cold water for 45–60 minutes or until they are pliable enough to wrap around your finger. But remember that they will still need some more cooking to truly soften. Drain.

In a small saucepan, gently heat the fish sauce, tamarind and palm sugar, just enough to dissolve the sugar. Taste and adjust the balance of flavour by adding more of any of those three ingredients. If you are using chilli, then add it at this point, then set the pad Thai sauce aside.

Place a wide, flat-bottomed pan or wok over high heat. Add 2 tablespoons of oil and get it singing hot. Add the garlic and fry for a few seconds in the hot oil. Add the noodles and a splash of water, then toss and stir-fry the noodles for a couple of minutes, coating them with the oil and garlic. Keep them moving in the pan. Add the pad Thai sauce and keep cooking until the noodles are almost soft enough to eat, but still a bit resistant to the bite.

Push the noodles to one side of the pan and add the prawns. Cook for a few seconds until they start to colour, then add the tofu. Once the prawns and tofu are both lightly browned, push them to one side as well. Now turn down the heat and add the eggs to the cleared space in the pan and scramble them gently.

When the eggs start to catch, add the dried shrimp, most of the spring onion and most of the peanuts to the pan and stir everything into the noodles, along with the prawns and tofu. Stir-fry until combined. Just before serving, throw in the bean shoots and the rest of the spring onion and peanuts.

Eat NOW, topped with sprigs of coriander and with the lime wedges on the side.

PERFECT WHITE FISH

Or, 20 not-so-secret (NSS) things that go really, really well with fish.

CITRUS

NSS #1: Sometimes a lemon wedge is all the dressing that fish needs, but there is so much more you can do with citrus. Think of 'cooking' your fish with lime juice to make a Peruvian ceviche or Fijian kokoda. Toss with either cubes of avocado or tomato before serving. Serve grilled fillets with a salad spiked with segments of pink grapefruit and pink peppercorns, or on a creamy, lemony sorrel purée. If you want to get more exotic try making an escabeche with orange and saffron.

DILL

NSS #2: Stuff whole fish for baking with dill stalks and lemon slices, sprinkle chopped dill into fish stews, use it when curing salmon for a gravlax, or just stir finely chopped dill into mayo as a simple dressing for any robust, flaky fish.

OLIVES

NSS #3: Dress baked chunky white fish fillets with a warm green olive vinaigrette or an anchovy-heavy black olive tapenade.

BUTTER

NSS #4: The delicate flesh of fish like snapper or whiting loves the gentle mantle of butter, whether in a lemon or white wine–hit beurre blanc or just as foaming butter spooned over in the pan. For bigger-flavoured white fish, like roasted blue eye or grilled sardines, think of ramping up the flavours with a beurre tomate (tangy tomato butter sauce) or a nut-brown butter.

POTATO

NSS #5: Cover a fish pie with mash, serve your battered flake with chips or top a fillet with delicate potato scales – any way at all, fish loves potato. Thicken a corn cob stock with cubes of potato for a seafood chowder or use leftover mash in fishcakes (salmon is great here). Or just buy some CHIPS!!!!!!!

PEAS

NSS #6: Fresh green peas with bacon make a wonderful base to sit under a fillet of roasted grouper or other chunky white fish. Blitz frozen peas with spring onions, oil and lemon juice for a silky purée, which will cook and sweeten as you warm it. Or go all Yorkshire and slow-cook mushy (ideally marrowfat) peas with butter and vinegar for your battered flake.

FENNEL (RICK STEIN MADE ME PUT THIS IN)

NSS #7: Roast fennel to serve with roasted blue eye; purée to serve under butter-poached or confit white fish or salmon; chop it finely to replace celery in the soffritto base for an Italian fish stew or pasta sauce. And spike that sauce or stew with a splash of Pernod or ouzo instead of wine, vermouth or verjuice, to help accent the aniseed flavour. Tarragon and dill bring a similar flavour hit.

LEEKS

NSS #8: While onions, garlic and spring onions all have their place with fish (oh my, how delicious is a fish pie made with an oniony sauce soubise!), I love the soft sweet creaminess of slow-cooked leeks even more. They accentuate the maritime salinity of the fish and the satin petals of its flesh; especially when the fish is pan-fried or roasted.

SHELLFISH

NSS #9: Whether it's a rich, ruddy bisque made from cray shells, an oil bronzed by roasted prawn heads or a mussel vinaigrette, remember to use all shellfish, from springy prawns to juicy pipis, for extra layers of texture and flavour in your fish dishes.

BACON

NSS #10: Lots of fishies love the smoky, porky saltiness of cured pork. Maybe I'm a fish? Try prosciutto-wrapped barramundi on the barbie or blue eye with bacon and a red wine sauce, like fish au vin.

COCONUT

NSS #11: The richness and creaminess of coconut goes really well with fish in Indian, Jamaican and South East Asian dishes, whether you are laying a barbecued fillet of salmon, barramundi or hapuka on a spiced coconut sauce or using a more robust fillet, like rockling or pink ling, to cook in a coconut-based curry sauce.

TOMATO

NSS #12: Roast them to serve with chunky roasted fish fillets, braise them with fish frames and crustacean shells to make the base for a fish soup or add the peeled, finely diced flesh to an oil and lemon vinaigrette along with basil and coriander seeds. This sauce vierge can be served warm or cold with delicate fish like whiting fillets. Tomato-based chilli, lime and coriander leaf salsa or a simpler, but hotter, Chilean pebre will do a similar job.

CAPERS

NSS #13: Use these brined or salted (and rinsed!) flower buds for oomphing up a vinaigrette for snapper fillets or adding depth to a meaty fish stew. Sprinkle crisp-fried capers over fish with butter sauce to cut the richness. And a lemon and caper butter is a joy all on its own when it comes to some perfectly cooked whiting fillets.

miso

NSS #14: Perfect whether you want to add a salty umami hit to your sauce or, even better, use it as the base for a sweet miso glaze over oily fish like toothfish or salmon.

FISH SAUCE

NSS #15: Some fish, prepared in certain ways, go well with the funky earthiness of fish sauce. Use it as the base for a palm sugar and lime dressing for a herb-laden salad under barbecued salmon or to add depth to your Thai fish curries. The same holds for adding anchovies to other Mediterranean flavours, like olives, tomatoes and capers.

PARSLEY

NSS #16: This versatile herb is perfect when blitzed with chilli and fresh coriander in a Moroccan chermoula. Rub onto chunky white fish fillets before baking or use as the base for a salsa verde to spoon onto robust fish.

GINGER

NSS #17: The heat and freshness of ginger just loves fish. Try baking salmon with honey, soy and fresh ginger, or serve fried blue eye with a dressing of sesame oil, red chilli and sweet kecap manis and topped with fried ginger strands. Steam a whole snapper with loads of ginger shreds, then dress it with sizzling peanut oil, soy and sliced spring onions. Or make a simple sauce with carrot or cucumber juice flavoured with ginger.

BREAD

NSS #18: Fishermen must have always had stale bread around, because every fishing village in the Mediterranean seems to marry fish with breadcrumbs. Try baking fillets of cheap white salmon with a parmesan and parsley-spiked breadcrumb crust, or fry butterflied sardines in a chunky breadcrumb coat. Or go all Turkish and make a sauce by pounding breadcrumbs with garlic, almonds and yoghurt.

SAMPHIRE & BEACH VEGETABLES

NSS #19 & 20: Try crispy baked or fried saltbush with salt and vinegar, the wet pop of pig face, or the greenest butter-warmed samphire spears as a sure-fire way to start your experimenting. Or just layer your fish on top of a veg-laden dashi. This simple broth can be bought in powdered form and is made from seaweed.

STEAMED FISH WITH CORIANDER, CASHEW AND LIME PESTO

Serves 2

Asian flavoured pesto with fish? Sure, any Genovese ancestors of mine, or yours, will be rotating in their graves even faster than a cricket ball out of Fawad Ahmed's right hand about now. But really … why not?

1 × 500 g or 2 × 250 g white fish fillets

PESTO
1 garlic clove, chopped
1 teaspoon grated ginger
1 bunch of coriander, leaves and stalks
3 tablespoons lime juice
  (roughly 1 ½ limes)
80 g (½ cup) unsalted cashews
½ teaspoon salt flakes
1 tablespoon vegetable oil

Blitz all the pesto ingredients in a food processor. (Yes, you can use a mortar and pestle if you feel that makes you more connected to the meal you are preparing with such lashings of love. I always feel that every time I let that pestle drop into that mortar I am saying 'I love you' to those I'm cooking for. BTW, did I tell you how much I like to cook with the seasons? And how my grandmother is my greatest inspiration in the kitchen? PS Can I have that cable cooking show now that I've mentioned all the required TV cook clichés???)

Taste the pesto and adjust the seasoning with a little bit more salt or lime juice.

Bring about 500 ml of water to a simmer in a large wok or saucepan, set over medium heat.

Line a large bamboo steamer basket with baking paper and place the fish on top. Cover the basket with a lid, then sit in the wok or pan over the water and cook for about 7 minutes, or until the fish is cooked through.

Top the fish with dollops of pesto and serve.

KINGFISH WITH CORIANDER, LIME, SOY AND JALAPEÑO

Serves 3–4 as a taster

I am not going to enter into the debate about whether Nobu Matsuhisa or Rainer Becker was first to champion the partnership of coriander and jalapeño in a Japanese environment, but I will say that I've tasted incarnations from both and both are eye-poppingly good. So, respect to them – and thanks for the inspiration for this dish, which I hope will allow home cooks like me to continue this most tasty of new traditions.

**1 lime, peeled and segmented,
 cut into tiny pieces**
1 tablespoon olive oil
220 g sashimi-grade kingfish
around 25 coriander leaves
**½ jalapeño chilli, deseeded, pith
 removed, diced as small as possible**
2 tablespoons soy sauce, for dipping

SPICY DRESSING
juice of 1 lime
½ bunch of coriander, leaves picked
1 jalapeño chilli
1 ½ teaspoons soy sauce
2 tablespoons good-quality mayonnaise

Toss the lime segments in the olive oil and leave them in a warm place for 15 minutes. This will take the sting out of the lime so you get the flavour without the acidity, which allows you to use more of it in the dish.

To make the spicy dressing, whiz up the lime juice, coriander leaves, chilli and soy sauce in a food processor. Measure 2 teaspoons into a separate bowl and stir in the mayonnaise to combine.

Cut the kingfish into 1 cm-thick slices. Arrange them on a serving plate and scatter on the lime segments, the coriander leaves and diced chilli. Dot small spoonfuls of spicy dressing around the plate and serve with the soy sauce on the side for dipping.

PUTTANESCA-BAKED WHITE FISH

Serves 2

This is the sort of dish you cook to share with someone you love. If I were into conceptual food, I'd tell you that the two white fish fillets represent the innocent calmness of lovers lying together and that the rich, intense sauce represents a world loaded and swirling with temptation and strong, heady distractions, but that instead of dividing the lovers, these things actually enhance their partnership.

But I'm not. I'm a home cook. So instead, I'll say that it's just about the tastiest thing you can do with a couple of hunks of white fish.

extra-virgin olive oil
salt flakes and freshly ground
   black pepper
2 × 180 g chunky white fish fillets
   (such as blue eye), all skin and bones
   removed

PUTTANESCA SAUCE
1 baby fennel bulb, finely sliced
   (fine young fronds reserved)
½ red onion, sliced
200 g cherry tomatoes, pierced
4 garlic cloves, smashed
salt flakes and freshly ground black
   pepper
6 thyme sprigs
2 ½ tablespoons extra-virgin olive oil
250 g (1 cup) crushed tomatoes
120 ml wine
1 ½ teaspoons sugar
1 ½ tablespoons red wine vinegar
70 g pitted kalamata olives
2 tablespoons capers,
   rinsed and drained

Preheat the oven to 200°C.

To make the puttanesca sauce, place the fennel, onion, cherry tomatoes and garlic in an oven-to-table baking dish. Season with salt and pepper and scatter on the thyme. Toss everything around in 2 tablespoons of the oil, then bake in the oven for 20 minutes. This lets you get a head start on the other ingredients that don't take as long.

Meanwhile, combine the crushed tomatoes, wine and sugar in a saucepan and bring to a simmer. Take the pan off the heat, stir in the vinegar and season just a little.

Pour the hot tomato sauce over the hot vegetables in the baking dish and scatter in the olives and capers.

Lightly oil and season the fish. Nestle each fillet down into the hot sauce in the oven-to-table baking dish, leaving the top of the fish just peeping through the sauce.

Bake for about 10 minutes. Don't overcook it! Remember that the fish will continue cooking in the hot sauce after it comes out of the oven. Sprinkle on the reserved fennel fronds and serve immediately.